Faith and Betrayal

Jean Rio

Faith and Betrayal

A Pioneer Woman's Passage
in the American West

SALLY DENTON

Alfred A. Knopf • New York • 2005

THIS IS A BORZOI BOOK
PUBLISHED BY ALFRED A. KNOPF

Copyright © 2005 by Sally Denton

All rights reserved under International and Pan-American Copyright
Conventions. Published in the United States by Alfred A. Knopf,
a division of Random House, Inc., New York, and simultaneously
in Canada by Random House of Canada Limited, Toronto.
Distributed by Random House, Inc., New York.

www.aaknopf.com

Knopf, Borzoi Books, and the colophon are
registered trademarks of Random House, Inc.

All photographs and illustrations are from the author's personal collection.

Library of Congress Cataloging-in-Publication Data

Denton, Sally.

Faith and betrayal : a pioneer woman's passage in the
American West / Sally Denton.—1st ed.

p.   cm.

Includes bibliographical references (p.) and index.

ISBN 1-4000-4135-X (alk. paper)

1. Rio, Jean, 1810–1883. 2. Ex-church members—Church of Jesus Christ
of Latter-day Saints—Biography. 3. Mormons—United States—
Biography. I. Title.

BX8678.R56D46 2005

978'.02'092—dc22   2004057742

[B]

Manufactured in the United States of America
First Edition

For Sara Kate, Leslie, Marianne,
and Jacqueline Denton,
Jean Rio's great-great-great-granddaughters
and keepers of her legacy

And he said to the woman,
Thy faith hath saved thee; go in peace.

Luke 7:50

CONTENTS

JEAN RIO'S FAMILY TREE

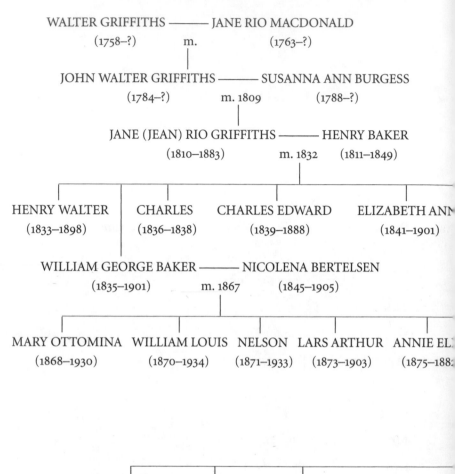

WALTER GRIFFITHS ——— JANE RIO MACDONALD
(1758–?)   m.   (1763–?)

JOHN WALTER GRIFFITHS ——— SUSANNA ANN BURGESS
(1784–?)   m. 1809   (1788–?)

JANE (JEAN) RIO GRIFFITHS ——— HENRY BAKER
(1810–1883)   m. 1832   (1811–1849)

HENRY WALTER   CHARLES   CHARLES EDWARD   ELIZABETH ANN
(1833–1898)   (1836–1838) (1839–1888)   (1841–1901)

WILLIAM GEORGE BAKER ——— NICOLENA BERTELSEN
(1835–1901)   m. 1867   (1845–1905)

MARY OTTOMINA WILLIAM LOUIS NELSON   LARS ARTHUR ANNIE EL
(1868–1930)   (1870–1934)   (1871–1933) (1873–1903) (1875–188

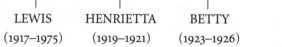

LEWIS   HENRIETTA   BETTY
(1917–1975)   (1919–1921)   (1923–1926)

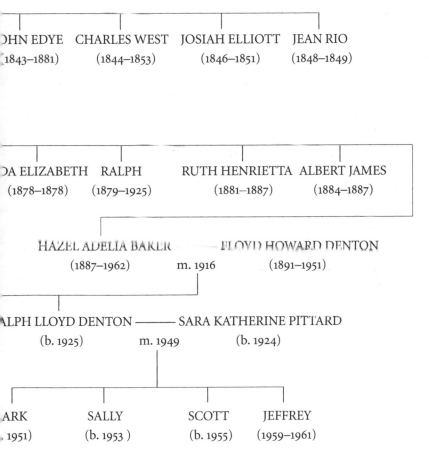

JHN EDYE   CHARLES WEST   JOSIAH ELLIOTT   JEAN RIO
(1843–1881)   (1844–1853)   (1846–1851)   (1848–1849)

DA ELIZABETH   RALPH   RUTH HENRIETTA ALBERT JAMES
(1878–1878)   (1879–1925)   (1881–1887)   (1884–1887)

HAZEL ADELIA BAKER ———— FLOYD HOWARD DENTON
(1887–1962)   m. 1916   (1891–1951)

ALPH LLOYD DENTON ——— SARA KATHERINE PITTARD
(b. 1925)   m. 1949   (b. 1924)

ARK   SALLY   SCOTT   JEFFREY
, 1951)   (b. 1953)   (b. 1955)   (1959–1961)

An Extraordinary Woman of Ordinary Virtues

My great-great-grandmother Jane (Jean) Rio Griffiths brought the first piano from England across the Great Plains and into the intermountain American West by wagon train in 1851. It was a feat that intrigued me as a little girl and young woman. But it was only later, when I explored her life, that I saw it was but one of her many accomplishments. Her spiritual passage was far more significant.

A recent convert to Mormonism, Jean Rio left an exceedingly comfortable life in London to make her way to the new Zion in the Great Salt Lake Valley of Utah Territory. Eventually, after a series of harrowing trials, physical and spiritual, she moved beyond the religiosity that had brought her to America, but she never lost faith in a higher spirituality, or in herself.

I was a teenager living in Boulder City, Nevada, when a distant relative—one of my father's cousins from a California branch of the family—arrived with a typed transcript of Jean Rio's diary, written in 1851. I was too young and too easily distracted then to follow up. The diary sat in my father's den, where, unbeknownst to me at the time, another version typed on faded onion skin rested unread in a box of papers that had belonged to my deceased paternal grandmother, Hazel Baker Denton. The provenance of these two copies of the diary is unclear. As it turned out, the Church of Jesus Christ of Latter-day Saints also had a copy of the same passages, as did a few of Jean Rio's descendants. Hundreds of pages of other relatives' diaries, letters, essays, and memoirs—portraying a tapestry of our family's history—had also been handed down to Hazel, the designated "writer" in the clan, and eventually these passed from her through her son, my father, to me.

It was only after I had become a journalist, ten years later, that I read Jean Rio's diary for the first time. But it would be years before I could turn my attention to her story in a deeper way. When I began my search I traveled to Denmark, England, Utah, California, and Nevada, gathering documents, oral histories, genealogical charts, letters, and newspaper articles. I found Jean Rio's crumbling gravestone in Antioch, California, and her magnificent piano in Salt Lake City—one of the few artifacts in the church-owned museum without an explanatory notice of how it was acquired.

Though Jean Rio left the Mormon faith disillusioned with its broken promises, the church continues to capitalize on her initial conversion and her contemporaneous emigration journal, even now displaying it, along with her piano, in an elaborate presentation at the temple in Salt Lake City. Sections of the diary were published during the twentieth century in various articles, books, church publications, and even the *Congressional Record.*

In fact, there are three different parts of Jean Rio's diary.

The first journal—what I call the emigration diary—details her journey from England to Utah during 1851 and the early months of her new life in Salt Lake City. The diary falls silent after March 1852 when Jean Rio's life becomes increasingly difficult under the theocracy of the Mormon Church. The entries briefly resume seventeen years later when she leaves Utah and resettles in California. The second—what I call the midwife's notebook—consists of fragmentary notations about births she attended between 1873 and 1881, after she had left Utah and the Mormon Church, and which I located during my research for this book. Finally, and perhaps most intriguing, on May 8, 1880, she added a small section to the end of the emigration diary regarding her decision to leave Utah. This section describes her one visit back to Utah during which she spent twenty-one months with her son William and his family. It includes a cryptic reference to what I call the California diary: "I have kept a daily diary a good deal of the time since I have been in California, which my children can refer to, if they wish." This journal has never surfaced.

The Mormon Church exploited her story, using the first part of the emigration version to promote its ideology, idealizing her as if she had remained among the faithful, excising the added portion of the diary that chronicled her break with it. Ironically, she who recorded history with such precision became part of the church's selective writing of history. Subsequent generations within her family—Mormon and non-Mormon alike—similarly embraced certain aspects of the diary that served their various interests. Mormon descendants of Jean Rio uphold the diary as evidence of a deeply spiritual woman devoted to the doctrines of the Church of Latter-day Saints, a woman who ultimately left Utah because of poverty rather than because of her overwhelming rejection of the church and its leaders. Non-Mormon descendants, like me, use the diary as evidence that, for many converts, the reality of nineteenth-century Utah—the church's expropriation of property under the doctrine of "consecration," the practice of polygamy, the violence of some of the rituals, all amid a dictatorial theocracy—was that of an oppressive regime, particularly for women.

The emigration diary—exceptional for its interpretation, analysis, description, and unfailing attention to the most mundane as well as the extraordinary details of daily life— breaks off abruptly in March 1852, when Jean Rio moves to Ogden amidst the fear and intimidation that has settled into the Mormon theocracy. The fact that she is apparently silent for the next seventeen years—until 1869 when she decides to abandon Utah—leaves us with a mystery. It is neither characteristic nor credible that a woman of such candor, literary acumen, and faithful journal-keeping, with such devotion to recording her daily life and the world around her, would have suddenly ceased writing at the moment of perhaps the most trying crisis of her life. Indeed, she makes clear that she continued a diary throughout the rest of her life. Where is that California diary? Were her papers and chronicles destroyed for the truths they revealed? Or did they simply disappear through the generations, as heirlooms are wont to do? In any case, I have reconstructed Jean Rio's life from the evidence that has survived.

"Women have not been well served in traditional assumptions about the American frontier," historian Ruth B. Moynihan has written. "Western mythology is replete with stereotypes about the active role of men and the symbolic function of women." Perhaps most starkly deficient in the portrayal by male historians is the character of the pioneering woman, who should be seen not as overworked helpmate but as adventure-seeking, nature-loving, courageous, talented, and free-spirited explorer of an uncultivated and untrammeled territory. "Pioneering is really a wilderness experience," observed a nineteenth-century woman immigrant. "We all need the wisdom of the wilderness—Moses did, Jesus did, and Paul did. The wilderness is the place to find God."

What impelled Jean Rio to leave her friends and most of her family behind in England, to travel thousands of miles across the Atlantic Ocean, and then to traverse thousands more miles of a partially uncharted country by steamship and ox-drawn wagon? What inspired her to forsake the silk sheets and court society of London for a faraway land unknown to her? What was the appeal to an elite English matron who seemingly had everything?

Jean Rio was born in 1810 and died in 1883. Through her diary we see and feel the expectation and wonder of coming to America, the sense of taking one's destiny into one's own hands, the thrill of exploring the wild and inspiring landscape of the Rocky Mountain West—a panorama we have seen largely through the eyes of men; the equally vivid accounts by women like Jean Rio have only recently begun to come to light. Without her diary, we would know virtually nothing of her life. Uncommon for its insight, observation, and sensibility, Jean Rio's account is, like many women's journals of the era, almost devoid of introspection. The emotions often seem diverted into descriptions of scenery that in its breathtaking splendor lends itself to the embellished prose.

From a stately London town house to a remote mountain valley in the fastness of the Rocky Mountains, Jean Rio persevered against seemingly insurmountable odds. She had a calling, and she was betrayed by the promises held out to her. But she found the strength and heroic bravery not simply to endure but to triumph. She rose to the challenges that confronted her—challenges that in many ways spanned the breadth of human experience, from the daily trials of sheer mortality to the larger tests of a changing society. While the scope of her experience, both the personal and the social, makes her an important example and metaphor for the modern woman, hers is but one of thousands of equally important stories of the women who settled the West, stories that provide a window on the capabilities of the human spirit. Jean Rio's story is but one exploration of the strengths of human nature that propel us forward in the midst of travail and hopelessness. This was a woman who chose her own path, regardless of the obstacles. While her adopted religion broke faith with her, she never failed to keep faith with herself.

Faith and Betrayal

CHAPTER ONE

"Worth a Long Walk to See"

SEPTEMBER 23, 1873. Jean Rio delivers the Ayer baby girl at five-fifteen p.m., after a relatively easy labor, and the mother sleeps quietly for the next several hours. "Had a good night," Jean Rio records in her midwife's notebook. ("The baby grows nicely [and] all seemed to enjoy themselves," she notes nearly a month later, after the mother brings the newborn and the rest of her children to pay a visit.)

It is not always as easy as it might seem. Even the uncomplicated births like Mrs. Ayer's are trials, the mother usually moaning and screaming in desperation through a long, painful labor to the final agony and then the sudden release of delivery. Often there are tests and horrors Jean Rio must face and somehow cope with, using only her hands and her self-taught skills, experience, and inherent fortitude—hemorrhaging or mortally ill mothers; distressed, deformed, or stillborn babies—a bloody life-and-death struggle no less of a test than any battle faced by a man.

When she cleans up afterward, changing one plain dress—now stained—for another, washing the blood and afterbirth from her hands and arms, she removes her rings, a fine gold

3

band and an exquisite small sapphire set in platinum. They are hardly the rings of a hardworking midwife on the raw California frontier of the late nineteenth century. She might seem a plain, even ordinary, woman of her time and place. But the unexpected grace and beauty of the rings match her own dignity and gentility. The rings signal that she is something other than an ordinary woman.

In her diary entry for October 23, she allows herself one of the rare references these days to the past that the rings echo. "Clear and lovely as a spring morning in England," she writes. "This summer was worth a long walk to see." How long a walk it has been, what a dramatic journey full of trust and betrayal, faith and disillusion, defeat and triumph, loss and gain! None of her new friends and neighbors in this rural hamlet can imagine it.

Only the rings and her obvious refinement and intellect, partially obscured by her unpretentious bearing, give a hint of the stark contrast between her past and present. Once she wore the finest gowns of European couture—a wardrobe so vast it had taken nearly an entire wagon to transport. Here she dresses in homespun. Once she performed the classics of song on the stages of Paris and London. Now she performs the exhausting rites of life and death, work no woman of her former station would have deigned to do. Most dramatically, once she was a prize convert to a powerful faith. Now she lives as a discreet fugitive from the betrayal of all that brought her here.

CHAPTER TWO

A Wine Cask on the Channel

TUMBRILS FILLED WITH entire families rolled along the cobblestone streets of Paris toward the guillotine amid howls and screams. All day, every day during 1792, the killing device was busy, corpses piling up faster than they could be disposed of. More than forty thousand people went to their deaths in those small carts. The decapitation was swift, taking less than half a second from the blade drop to the rolling head—the guillotine was "an instrument adopted by the Revolutionists for the more scientific and humane beheading of the condemned." Almost all the members of the Rio family from Lamballe, Brittany—renamed Côtes-du-Nord by the revolutionary government—were among them. "Hourly, the hideous instrument of torture claimed its many victims— old men, young women, tiny children—until the day when it would finally demand the head of a King and of a beautiful young Queen," as one fictional account put it.

Entire generations were eliminated, as victims of all ages were placed facedown on a bench. "The mechanism falls like lightning; the head flies off; the blood spurts; the man no longer exists," Dr. Joseph-Ignace Guillotin once explained to a nervous audience. The instrument, however, wasn't always that efficient.

Many of the Rios, like thousands of others, had tried to flee—to England, Belgium, Scotland, Holland, Canada, or the United States. At least one small Rio girl would be delivered from the bloodbath.

In Paris in the summer of 1789, during the earliest phase of the French Revolution—the "Great Fear"—a manservant long devoted to a wealthy French couple from the Rio clan placed their infant daughter in a wine cask. Thus concealed, the baby was smuggled across the English Channel. Her parents and every known family member are believed to have stayed behind, and to have become victims of the revolutionists. Once in England, the guardian christened his tiny refugee with the name Susanna Ann Burgess while providing her with protection in a new land. The fabricated surname, according to family lore, denoted the bourgeois roots of her family, though the reality no doubt was more complicated. The two made their way to Scotland, to the Isle of Skye, where relatives and royalist sympathizers embraced the child. They remained in hiding as the London society press regularly reported on new arrivals from France. The English response to the events taking place across the Channel vacillated between horror and sympathy, trepidation at the infectious revolutionary spirit, and base curiosity.

Susanna would spend her childhood and adolescence in Scotland, her guardian impressing upon her a deep hatred of all things French. This was the story Jean Rio told her children and grandchildren about her French and Scottish ancestors and her mother's flight from persecution to freedom. She apparently never imparted information about the origins of her own middle name, Rio, perhaps embarrassed by the aristocratic association.

At the time of the revolution, France was the wealthiest and most powerful nation in the world. Its society was divided into three classes. The First Estate—the clergy—controlled the press, monopolized religion, governed the educational institutions, and owned the choice land. The Second Estate consisted of the nobility, who were exempt from taxation but held all high government positions. The Third Estate was the class that encompassed the remaining 98 percent of the population and included the bourgeoisie, the proletariat, and the peasantry. Judging from Susanna Burgess's entrée into elite, if not noble, society in Scotland, her parents were most likely either nobility or part of the educated upper middle class that sympathized with the Second Estate rather than the masses. With the Third Estate uprising on July 14, 1789, which destroyed the Bastille prison, symbol of royal tyranny, nobles and members of the upper bourgeoisie fled for their lives. The early-twentieth-century novelist Baroness Emmuska Orczy immortalized the flight in *The Scarlet Pimpernel:* "Men in women's clothes, women in male attire, children disguised in beggars' rags. In various disguises, under various pretexts, they tried to slip through the barriers, which were so well guarded by citizen soldiers of the Republic."

Susanna would be one of thousands of French émigrés to

England during the last decade of the eighteenth century, a time when open boats laden with refugees often navigated the stormy Channel in darkness. Many, like Susanna, were babies entrusted by their doomed parents to lowly retainers who had no price on their heads. "The English never ceased to wonder at the degree of devotion manifested by the servants of the French émigrés, greatly admiring their unalterable attachment to their masters," according to a twentieth-century British scholar of the period. While the identity neither of the servant nor of Susanna's parents is known, it is assumed her parents and all of her siblings were executed during the Reign of Terror, which started less than two years after Susanna's flight to Scotland. When Napoléon rose to power a decade later and announced he would welcome back his nation's exiles, Susanna and her guardian chose not to return.

The themes inherent in Susanna's escape from Jacobin France would eerily be echoed in her daughter Jean Rio's life: privilege, persecution, flight, liberation, and concealment. Susanna was born into a family of privilege and forced to escape when the social order collapsed. Jean Rio was moved to flee by a different kind of oppression, what she saw as spiritual bankruptcy. In the end, they both found refuge in hiding.

In 1809, at the age of twenty, Susanna Ann Burgess married a well-to-do Scotsman named John Walter Griffiths, four years older than she and descended from Scottish aristocracy. John's father could trace his roots back several generations in London, with family christenings and marriages recorded for centuries at the same historic church. John's mother, Jane Rio MacDonald, was of the landed-gentry MacDonald clan on the Isle of Skye, the MacDonalds having arrived in Scotland from the southern Hebrides in the thirteenth century. Her middle name would seem to indicate a relationship through blood and class lines to Susanna's French family. In 1790 Lord Mac-Donald, either a brother or a cousin to Jane Rio MacDonald, built Armadale Castle on his 200,000-acre Highland estate, where the famous Scottish Jacobite Flora Macdonald had married and where, in 1746, she had hidden Prince Charles Edward, Bonnie Prince Charlie, from Hanoverian troops. "With a price of thirty pounds on his head, he [Prince Charles Edward] wandered hungry and sick from one sanctuary to another, endangering everyone who gave him shelter," one historian wrote. Flora Macdonald disguised him as an Irish maidservant and facilitated his escape to the mainland. The MacDonalds' political and social circles included such luminaries as Samuel Johnson and James Boswell, indicating that John Griffiths was born and bred in a lofty world.

While a scion of Scottish nobility like John Griffiths might have fallen in love with and wed the supposed daughter of a fugitive French servant, the class lines and social conventions of the time make such a match highly improbable. The conjecture of genealogists and descendants rests on the more likely scenario that John and his distinguished family recognized Susanna as an aristocratic orphan and political refugee, if not a distant Rio cousin. All involved would have kept such a fact discreetly concealed in the still-charged atmosphere of the Napoleonic years, when escapees from the guillotine might still be prey to some settling of old scores.

The patrician Rio family dated back to the late sixteenth century in the renamed Côtes-du-Nord. Sparsely populated by nobles, priests, and peasants, the region was virtually devoid of the rising middle class. Its inhabitants were passionately loyal to the Catholic monarchy, an antirevolutionary stronghold. Entrenched Catholicism dating back to the fourth century fueled a zealotry and isolationism that kept the nobility out of touch with the object of the revolution. The area would come to symbolize some of the most ruthless reprisals and cold-blooded massacres perpetrated by the revolutionaries. "The worst excesses were committed in the provinces," historian Christopher Hibbert writes of the bloodshed. "In several towns the guillotine was kept constantly at work and those convicted of crimes against the Revolution were slaughtered wholesale."

The Rio family had greatly diminished by the end of the eighteenth century, and in the nineteenth century only a handful of Rio births were recorded in France. The name became so rare that it could soon be traced only to an extremely wealthy Rio clan in rural Chard, England, and to the family of Susanna Burgess's new mother-in-law on the Isle of Skye. Genealogical records and documents relating to Susanna Burgess give her birthdate only as "about 1788" and contain no further details as to place of birth, baptism, or pedigree.

When, on May 8, 1810, Susanna gave birth to her only child, she chose an anglicized spelling for her daughter's name—

Jane instead of the French Jeanne. Eventually the name would become Jean. The Rio name, pronounced with a long *i* and sometimes spelled "Rioux," would be carried forward when Jean Rio's firstborn son would include the name in that of each of his eight children.

John and Susanna's daughter, Jean Rio Griffiths, would be baptized in London at the St. Lawrence Jewry, an impressive structure built in the twelfth century and dedicated to the martyr who had been roasted alive on a gridiron in third-century Rome. Rebuilt in 1670 by the great English architect Sir Christopher Wren, it was adorned with gold-leaf chandeliers, Grinling Gibbons carvings, and a window commemorating its pre-Reformation preacher, the martyred St. Thomas More. The rituals performed in this imposing edifice, a flagship of the Anglican establishment, would shape and dominate the first forty years of Jean Rio's religious and spiritual life.

Jean Rio was born near the Jewry, in the district where William the Conqueror had relocated Jews in the eleventh century, and she would grow up an only child in the neighborhood of the Jewry and in the shadow of London's Guildhall, the center of city government since the Middle Ages and during her lifetime a massive library. Though an intellectual life was largely reserved for males in the England of her youth, Jean Rio's prosperous parents—both highly educated—afforded her every opportunity for learning. Professors of music came to their home to teach her to play the harp and the piano. She was granted an early education and she became an avid reader at a time when girls of her class were ridiculed for intellectualism. "As a rule, when girls had left school they were thought to be wasting time if seen reading," wrote one of Jean Rio's British contemporaries. "They were allowed to spend their superfluous energy in fancy work, and ridiculous wax-flower making, without molestation; but 'put down your book,' and 'don't waste your time that way,' were common expressions." Perhaps owing to her parents' Scottish ancestry, books were a valued part of Jean Rio's life. Early on, "reading and writing became embedded in Scottish society," according to historian Arthur Herman. In Edinburgh "there were six publishing houses in 1763, for a city with a population of only sixty thousand." She was educated in the English classics and had the good fortune to live at a time when four of the greatest British novelists were women. The fictional spheres of Jane Austen, George Eliot, and Emily and Charlotte Brontë were representative of Jean Rio's own rarefied world.

Unlike reading, music was considered appropriate for pubescent girls as what a nineteenth-century writer called "the least thought-inspiring" avenue to "soothe the savage breast." Commonly, parents of this era who dissuaded their daughters from highbrow pursuits and development fostered by books thought it "no waste of time," as one observer noted, "for them to spend two or three hours a day at the piano." Eventually Jean Rio studied at a conservatory, though we don't know which one. Her career as a singer and pianist then took her to concert halls in Paris, Madrid, and Milan.

Other than her emigration diary, which was written as a letter home to a close friend, as well as brief remarks in her later midwife's notebook, no additional examples of her own writing are known to exist.

She married Henry Baker of London on September 24, 1832, in the St. Lawrence Jewry, where her mother had married her father and her paternal grandmother had married her grandfather. The twenty-two-year-old newlywed presided over a house on Lake Street near St. Paul's Cathedral. She gave birth to her first child, Henry Walter, the following summer. Two years after the first baby, she gave birth to William George in 1835. Her third son, Charles, died as a toddler, and in 1839 she christened her fourth son Charles Edward. Elizabeth Ann was born in 1841, John Edye in 1843, Charles West in 1844, Josiah Elliott in 1846, and Jean Rio in 1848.

Child rearing was left to governesses, and the children were taught what one of them called "the pure Queen's English" by private tutors, as Jean Rio pursued her musical career throughout Europe. A cook and butler handled domestic matters, and Jean Rio and Henry took their meals separate from the children. The family regularly attended public celebrations for Queen Victoria, and, to judge from their proximity to the royal family at these times, the Bakers were apparently among the elite of mid-nineteenth-century London society.

Henry, a prominent engineer, built a miniature steam locomotive for his children. The couple routinely read Shakespeare aloud to their children from a leather-bound volume of the complete works—a book Jean Rio would eventually carry with her to Utah, along with many others. "They were taught personal cleanliness, morals, manners, and religion in no uncer-

tain terms," wrote a descendant. As each child turned fourteen, he or she was invited to the family dinner table, having
received training in etiquette. At that age, the sons were presented with a silver watch and chain. By that age as well, the
children were expected to have mastered the common require-
ments in history and literature, as well as bookkeeping and
higher mathematics that included algebra. Upon turning sixteen, the boys received a gold watch and, as son William
George remembered the symbolic rite, were told by Jean Rio
and Henry that they would now be expected to conduct themselves as proper gentlemen at all times. All the children learned
horsemanship and regularly rode the bridle path in Hyde
Park; it was a proficiency that would serve them well in their
future lives on the American frontier.

In 1840, Jean Rio's paternal great-uncle, William Rio Mac-
Donald, bequeathed a substantial amount of property and
cash to her. MacDonald, who had been surgeon to the king,
had resided at 46 Doughty Street, one of London's most
famous Georgian avenues. At the time of MacDonald's death,
the neighborhood was at the heart of the city's literary life;
that year Charles Dickens moved with his wife into the house
next door. Among the property listed in MacDonald's will
along with the Doughty Street residence were "leaseholds" in
Tabernacle Walk and Rose Court. Also bequeathed to Jean Rio
were a home on Chiswell Street and all its "appurtenances,"
the rents and profits from numerous other properties, and an
annuity for the rest of her life, all "free from the control, debts,
or engagements of her husband."

Whether the family relocated from their Lake Street home

to Doughty Street is unclear, but what is obvious is that Jean Rio Baker was a very wealthy woman in her own right by 1840. As she was living at the height of comfort, however, England was experiencing the most severe depression of the century. Since losing the American War of Independence, Great Britain had been in crisis. "Its politics were stuck in permanent factionalism and gridlock," writes Arthur Herman. "A sense of malaise had settled over its ruling class, while popular unrest, encouraged by the French Revolution, spread across the provinces."

Throughout the 1840s, the poverty and degradation brought about by the Industrial Revolution became more and more staggering, as depicted so famously by Charles Dickens in *Oliver Twist* and other novels of life in Victorian England. Women and children had entered the workforce in record numbers, and most of them suffered abhorrent factory conditions and earned a pittance for a backbreaking day's work. People of various races and cultures were flocking to London in search of employment with the railways and shipyards, the new city-dwellers living in wretched conditions. Bedraggled children toiled for fourteen hours a day in factories; squalid brothels bred disease; the slums were awash in sewage; and there was a burgeoning criminal population. The grim deaths from the Irish famine that began with the blight of the potato crop in 1845 dominated the London newspapers, and Ireland was poised for violent revolution.

At the same moment, the Church of England was in a crisis of its own, as reformers increasingly sought a separation between church and state. All the critics seemed to agree that neither the church nor the government was adequately addressing the appalling social conditions. "When the inner cities are crying out, what are the [Ecclesiastical] Commissioners doing? They bought a palace for the Bishop of Gloucester and Bristol, lots of bedrooms," British scholar Owen Chadwick writes of the rising tide of dissent and suspicion. As the populace increasingly protested the church's corruption—bishops were burned in effigy and crowds called for Canterbury Cathedral to be turned into stables—politicians began pushing for reform to pacify a restless nation.

The Church of England stubbornly resisted the oncoming changes, providing a wedge for the evangelicals who were transforming the European and American religious landscapes. "Its piety tended to be sober, earnest, dutiful, austere, or even prosaic in expression," Chadwick observes of the church at that time. Meanwhile, the evangelicals "preached their way into the hearts of rich and poor, neglectful of parish boundaries, friendly with dissent." Rejecting the staid, authoritarian dogma of the past, this faction encouraged believers to choose feeling over thinking in their path to God. "Romantic literature and art, the sense of affection and the sensibility of beauty pervading European thought, the flowering of poetry, the medievalism of the novel or of architecture," as Chadwick describes the new arousal, posed a threat to church conservatives. The evangelicals brought poverty, corruption, and injustice to the forefront of the national dialogue as part of the New Age movement to elevate society, and advocated a Christian Socialism that predated Marxist and other socialist phenomena in politics.

For all the world's "progress," in the first half of the nineteenth century the sense of the precariousness and fragility of life was keen, the populace at the mercy of a physical world of microbes and human physiology still little understood. Epidemics of cholera, typhoid, and influenza decimated entire cities. What a century later would be relatively minor diseases and accidents, at least in Europe and the United States, were often lethal. Children died of afflictions as common as runny noses and diarrhea. Slight wounds turned gangrenous and fatal. Congenital deformities and genetic diseases beyond any treatment seemed the vengeance of an unpredictable God. Even for Jean Rio, a privileged woman with servants, it was a life with its share of hardship and uncertainty. Like her peers, she was raised to fear and worship God, to see religion as the only true deliverance from life's random travails.

In this era, one's faith was defining, and it was expressed fulsomely, without shame or embarrassment. Agnostics and atheists were rare. Charles Darwin had not yet written *The Origin of Species* challenging the simplistic biblical view of Creation. True believers accepted the Bible in literal terms— "felt as close to Abraham, Isaac, Jacob and a host of other characters as they did to their own friends and relatives," according to J.R.H. Moorman—and thought the Scriptures were infallible.

Jean Rio saw the degraded condition of British life as a clear sign of the approaching end-time in biblical terms—a millennial expectancy creating a groundswell at the time. Offended by the greedy, uncaring attitude of a Church of England that defied reform, she sought a different path to spiritual salvation. Of keen intellect and compassion, hers would be a fecund mind for Mormon persuasion.

Just as the Church of England was steeped in corruption and slow to recognize its crippling social irrelevance, religion in mid-nineteenth-century America was facing its own upheavals and transformations. With the evangelical movement of the 1820s, a rousing and muscular new spirituality had swept over most of the major denominations of America. New sects and new approaches were challenging the Congregationalists, Presbyterians, and others to faith and ritual. The Church of Jesus Christ of Latter-day Saints was one of the many fledgling and often transitory movements born in the turbulence of the moment, a moment of frontier revivals, spiritual visitations, and widespread belief in magic and the occult. Growing out of this wider impulse, the Mormon Church as envisioned by its prophet and founder was to be a cooperative theocracy responsive to the social and spiritual needs of all mankind. Above all, the new religion was rooted in the fervent notion that the "latter days" were indeed at hand.

Fueled by millennialist passions for deliverance and everlasting life, Mormonism was born in a time known as the Second Great Awakening. It was conceived by a charismatic young American farmer named Joseph Smith, who claimed to have had a vision in 1823 in which an illuminated angel named Moroni directed him to excavate some ruins near his home in Palmyra, in western New York. Smith said Moroni visited him three times and told him that God had selected him to restore the one true church in North America in preparation for the Second Coming of Christ. His first job, Smith said he was told, was to find a book inscribed on golden plates that Moroni had buried in nearby Cumorah fourteen centuries earlier. To assist Smith in translating the "reformed Egyptian" symbols on the tablets would be two crystal seer stones, the Urim and Thummim, buried with the sacred texts.

The self-proclaimed prophet said he located and unearthed these golden plates on the designated night of September 22, 1827. He was then twenty two. He said that by using the magic stones he was able to decipher the mysterious engravings, dictating the stories contained on the leaves to assistants. By April 1829, Smith, who was illiterate, had completed a 275,000-word manuscript. This *Book of Mormon,* named for the ancient military figure who Smith believed led the first emigrants from Palestine to North America, was said to be based upon the journal of Mormon's son, Moroni, the last diarist of the supposedly historic events.

Full of heroes and villains, bloodshed and miracles, warriors and intrigue, rich biblical symbols and autobiographical themes, the narrative was a revised and enhanced New Testament, and it included the details of a journey to America by Christ immediately after his resurrection to visit his chosen people. The book depicted a Hebrew tribe led by a man called Lehi, who had left Jerusalem in 600 BC and sailed to the Americas with his six sons and other followers. Once there, Smith wrote, the tribe broke into two warring factions: the devout and godly under the good son, Nephi; the evil sinners under the bad seed, Laman. God was seen as blessing the Nephites and all of their descendants with white skin, while cursing the violent Lamanites with dark skin. The "white and delightsome" Nephites battled the bloodthirsty Lamanites for six hundred years, until Christ rose from the dead, turned up in North America to preach to these displaced Palestinians, and persuaded each side to abandon its barbarous ways. The tale of the Nephites and the Lamanites explained the "Hebraic" origin of Native Americans, a popular theory of the day—that the Indians of North America were a remnant of the mythical lost tribes of Israel, and must therefore be "gathered" in anticipation of Christ's return. "The theory that the Americans are of Jewish origin has been discussed more minutely and at greater length than any other," writes the historian H. H. Bancroft.

Reflective of the mystical leanings of the era, the *Book of Mormon* was an unsophisticated view of the clash between good and evil. At the core was a belief that all churches had deviated from the true theology of Christianity—what Smith called the "Great Apostasy"—and that Smith's divine task was to gather the remnants of Israel to a latter-day Zion and await the millennium. Central to the theology was a conviction that all male devotees were on the road to godhood, that all men could create their own worlds, and that all women, if pure and obedient to men, could be "pulled through the veil" to this kingdom as eternal companions to righteous men.

Smith published the *Book of Mormon* in 1830. It not only became a best seller, it also created an entirely new and exciting theology. With himself at the helm as "Prophet, Seer, and Revelator," Smith immediately assembled a church with six followers. A month later the ranks would swell to forty, and more than a thousand would be converted within a year. Denouncing the "false spirits" common to the post–Revolutionary War revivalism of the day, Smith spoke of ongoing, regular contact between God and men, and the seductive notion that humans could be creators of their own worlds. He contended that his divine revelations evidenced his infallibility, his entire religion having been based upon miracles that defied secular challenge. Neither Luther nor the Pope had spoken directly to God, Smith said in countering his critics, while he professed to have had more than a hundred personal conversations with God.

Founding his Church of Jesus Christ of Latter-day Saints, he created an evangelical socialism ruled by an autocratic cadre of "worthy males" and based on a theology of the fast-approaching end-time as prophesied in the Bible's Book of Revelation. "In no other period in American history were 'the last days' felt to be so imminent," Smith biographer Fawn Brodie puts it, "as in that between 1820 and 1845." The earth was thought to be nearing six thousand years old, according to scientific calculations then current, and since biblical references suggested that a thousand years was a single day to God, many of the world's religious leaders put the earth's impending seventh day—the "day of rest and peace" when Christ would descend—at some point in the mid-1800s. "The literalist Mormon timetable counts forward from the first six 'days' of Genesis," writes James Coates, "and the seventh day of a thousand years when God rested after Adam and Eve began their time in Eden." Smith's apocalyptic vision included the fall of all churches and governments, which would leave his own theocracy as the ruling government of the world.

Early Mormonism held a number of fundamental beliefs, controversial among mainstream Christians at the time, that would find expression in the swelling New Age spiritual movement that began late in the twentieth century. The divine power of crystals, personal transformation, channeling, divination, astrology, holistic health, and the allegiance to a new world order all had credence in Joseph Smith's religion. "Mormonism is an eclectic religious philosophy, drawn from Brahmin mysticism in the dependence of God, the Platonic and Gnostic notion of Eons, . . . Mahomedan sensualism, and the fanaticism of the sects of the early church . . . with the convenient idea of the transmigration of souls, from the Persian," concluded a firsthand observer of the new phenomenon.

Smith's homegrown American gospel that denied original sin and provided a road to godhood for the individual was a religious version of the American dream that defied the Calvinist vision of a vengeful God. In a culture in which parents and teachers told their boys they could grow up to be president, Smith held out to his flock the promise that they could become gods. Unlike any other creed in the United States, Mormonism, neither Judaic nor traditional Christian, maintained a strong cerebral appeal throughout its early years. "Joseph had convincing answers to the thorniest existential questions," wrote Jon Krakauer in 2003—answers that were both explicit and comforting. "He offered a crystal-clear notion of right and wrong, an unambiguous definition of good and evil."

It would not be until twentieth-century science and scholarship debunked many of Smith's claims that the theology itself would be widely ridiculed. Even its more controversial doctrine of polygamy found sanction in the Old Testament. By 1832 Smith had sent missionaries to evangelize throughout the eastern states. They preached "the Kingdom is come, glory hallelujah," and met with unparalleled success. Smith began searching for a locale to build the "Kingdom of God upon Earth."

As the numbers of converts grew, Smith moved his new church from New York State to Kirtland, Ohio, where his disciples converted and baptized the entire community. The once-humble Smith transformed himself into a powerful prophet and dictator, coming into increasing conflict with many of his neighbors and followers. Americans passionate about their new democracy found Smith's theocracy outlandish if not threatening. Nearly all of his high-ranking churchmen fell out with him over his authoritarian rule, and his inner circle began to fade away. Smith said he then received a revelation from God that in order to save his church he must pursue converts in Great Britain who had been cradled with kings.

His most charismatic apostles were chosen for this foreign mission, including one named Brigham Young, who performed nine missions between 1832 and 1837. Throughout England, Scotland, and Wales, they converted hundreds and then thousands, and they organized what would become a massive emigration system. The missionaries' teachings centered upon a mixture of Bible texts on "the earth's final days," prophesies about the millennium, the return of the Jews to Palestine, the resurrection of the dead, and, especially, the rise of the new prophet Joseph Smith. "There is a strange power with them that fascinates the people and draws them into their meshes in spite of themselves," wrote a British woman who fell sway to the missionaries during this time. The missionaries found the English manufacturing towns a fertile field, populated as they were with poor, ignorant, and superstitious laborers susceptible to hopeful stories of miracles.

In London, the missionaries appealed to a wealthy educated class that had been swept up by the religious skepticism of the earlier Age of Reason as epitomized by England's own Thomas Paine (who emigrated to America in 1774). The erudite, like Jean Rio Baker, saw the establishment Church of England as an obstacle to social change and eagerly welcomed an American reform religion in its place. Seen as the gospel of Christianity restored, early Mormonism captivated the minds of some of the more religiously inclined. The doctrines that would later be so contested and seen as so loathsome by the more cerebral converts—polygamy, "blood atonement" (the killing of sinners), priestly theocracy—were not mentioned by these early missionaries. Instead, the missionaries focused on the "good news" of the everlasting Gospel—repentance, baptism, and faith—and made the new religion sound fresh and progressive.

CHAPTER THREE

These Latter Days

WHILE PROSELYTIZING EFFORTS abroad were over-whelmingly successful, the Latter-day Saints, as Smith had christened his flock, were met with increasing scorn and derision in the United States. Mormonism had become America's most controversial, clannish, imperialistic religion. Setting his followers apart, calling all non-Mormons "Gentiles," claiming to be the leader of God's chosen people, espousing a collectivism that was anathema to the rollicking capitalism of the day, Smith seemed to encourage and thrive on the condemnation and persecution that greeted his sect. Mormonism's unabashed devotion to material wealth stood in stark contrast to the asceticism of other denominations, and what seemed to many a too-naked prosperity-as-godliness mentality offended neighbors who belonged to traditional Christian denominations—the Presbyterians and Methodists. Conflicts in Ohio between Mormons and local "Gentiles" erupted into violence, and when the church-owned bank went broke a warrant was issued for Smith's arrest on charges of fraud. Before Smith could face those allegations, God, he said, revealed to him that the new Zion was not in Ohio after all, but in Far West, Missouri—the site, said Smith, of the original Garden of Eden. Fleeing in the middle of the night, Smith rode his horse eight hundred miles west to the newly designated Promised Land.

It would not be long before the Mormons alienated Missourians as well, with tensions increasing as thousands of new converts poured into the community and especially as vague rumors of polygamy evolved into hard evidence of ubiquitous plural marriages. The clashes would culminate in what would become known as the "extermination order," in which Missouri's governor, Lillburn W. Boggs, claimed that "Mormons must be treated as enemies and must be exterminated or driven from the state, if necessary, for the public good." They would move on to yet another so-called Zion in Nauvoo, Illinois.

Arriving in 1839 at the picturesque town on the eastern bank of the Mississippi River, the thirty-three-year-old Smith set out with a grandiose vision to build the country's wealthiest and most powerful separatist city-state, which he said was ordained by God, a model theocracy to rival Washington. By this time the Mormon militia—Smith's "Army of God," with Smith as commander in chief—was nearly one-quarter the size of the U.S. Army. Less than a decade after founding his church, Smith had lured thousands of Europeans to make perilous Atlantic crossings and arduous journeys across one-third of the American continent to Illinois, while also attracting adherents in his own country. Marked by disillusionment with the old faiths and profound yearning for both the temporal security and the eternal salvation offered by Mormonism, poor Americans also were enamored with the promise. Though

Smith said there had been earlier divine revelations ordaining polygamy, it would be here, in Nauvoo, where the "Law of Jacob," as the doctrine of multiple marriage was called, was officially added to the Mormons' distinctive practices. That principle, more than all else, would irrevocably alienate the Mormons from their Protestant neighbors.

Advocating theocratic rule for the entire nation, Smith announced his candidacy for the U.S. presidency in 1844. Prophesying the impending overthrow of the national government, he began acting with increasing recklessness, inspiring even more hostility toward him and what was now seen by many as his peculiar cult. Covertly married to nearly fifty wives, Smith faced rampant defections from his ranks on the issue of polygamy. In the summer of 1844 he declared martial law in his independent city-state, as well-armed anti-Mormon mobs gathered near Nauvoo. Smith would be arrested for destroying the offices of a newspaper that had published exposés on polygamy, and on the morning of June 27, 1844, he would be shot to death in a Carthage, Illinois, jail by vigilantes. Smith was the first American religious leader ever to be assassinated, and to his followers, his martyrdom was on a par with that of Jesus Christ.

A chaotic succession crisis ensued, as more than a dozen cabals sought to take over Smith's reign. Internal struggles briefly threatened the stability of the church. But by August 8, 1844, the blustering apostle Brigham Young had unofficially but unmistakably seized control. "Young arose and roared like a young lion," recalled a devoted "Saint" (as followers now called themselves), who said Young not only imitated the style

and voice of Smith but was enveloped in Smith's unique illuminated aura as well. For the next thirty-three years Young
would lead his growing congregation with a discipline and
rigor of historic proportions.

Born June 1, 1801, Young was raised in the same milieu as
Smith—the period of religious revival sweeping the eastern
states. The son of impoverished dirt farmers, Young learned
the carpenter's trade as an adolescent and crafted primitive
furniture that he sold door to door. He noticed that many of his
neighbors and relatives were influenced by the *Book of Mormon*, and by 1832 he had abandoned carpentry to begin proselytizing for Joseph Smith's new church. Wholly uneducated
but swift of mind, Young rose quickly in Smith's capricious
hierarchy as he threw himself into the missionary enterprise. A
passionate convert from the start, Young had set out—"without purse or scrip," as the missionaries were expected to do—
with a zealous commitment to the doctrine of spiritual and
physical gathering of Saints to Zion. "Every sentiment and feeling should be to cleanse the earth from wickedness, purify the
people, sanctify the nations, gather the nations of Israel home,
redeem and build up Zion, redeem Jerusalem and gather the
Jews there, and establish the reign and kingdom of God on
earth," Young said of his calling as a Mormon evangelist.

By the time of Smith's death, Young had served ten missions, including stints in Canada, the eastern states, and Great
Britain. He had reported seeing angels in 1835 and was
acknowledged as a "Prophet and Seer" in 1836; he would not
proclaim himself a "Revelator" until a few years later, when he

claimed to have received a divine revelation that he should lead his people out of Nauvoo to the Great Salt Lake Valley.

Independent, outspoken, stubborn, arrogant, vengeful, and hot-tempered, the unabashed polygamist antagonized his "Gentile" neighbors as thoroughly and dangerously as had Smith. Marrying forty times, in violation of Illinois law, he was forced into hiding by 1845 to avoid numerous legal writs. Young established "a police state in Nauvoo," according to one of his biographers, Stanley P. Hirshson; he "strapped on a pair of six-shooters and vowed he would kill any man who handed him another summons or grabbed hold of him."

Young knew that the survival of his sect depended upon finding a homeland west of the Rocky Mountains and outside the boundaries of the United States. He began studying the reports and maps of explorers John C. Frémont and Lansford W. Hastings, and he decided on land in the Great Basin that then belonged to Mexico as a site for the new Zion. Arid and desolate, this section of the Great American Desert was thought to be incapable of sustaining a large population. But Young was attracted to its harshness, its frigid winters, its scorching summers, and its brief growing season as an environment too unfriendly and challenging for his enemies to crowd him. Here, finally, the Latter-day Saints could build their "Kingdom of God upon Earth," a theocracy outside the purview of the judgmental and menacing Americans, isolated by the indomitable Rocky Mountains to the east and the Sierra Nevada to the west.

Called "the Lion of God" for his zeal in moving the Saints

out of Illinois and into the new Zion, Young accomplished what has been hailed as the emigration feat of the age. His hegira ended in July 1847 in a place the Mormons would name Deseret. With great force and drive, Young ushered his tired and persecuted Saints to their homeland. "The prophet, through the sheer force of his personality, led, goaded, threatened, fought, pummeled, cajoled, and otherwise drove the thousands of Mormon men, women, and children through the wilderness to an American Canaan called Utah on the shores of an inland Dead Sea called the Great Salt Lake," writes James Coates, drawing an unmistakable parallel to Moses.

It would be Young who turned the Mormons into the most resourceful and disciplined pioneers in American history. Alongside Manifest Destiny and the California gold rush, the evangelical energy of the mid-nineteenth century, of which Mormonism was representative, was significant in colonizing the American frontier. Brilliant and resourceful, Young realized that the rugged, snow-capped mountains encircling Deseret could provide a bounteous supply of water. Under Young's direction, the Saints diverted the spring runoff into ditches and canals that lured the water into the desert. Creating a complex and ambitious irrigation system never before seen in the West, they soon had the previously barren desert floor covered with productive fields. "In the New World," writes Marc Reisner in *Cadillac Desert,* "Indians had dabbled with irrigation, and the Spanish had improved their techniques, but the Mormons attacked the desert full-bore, flooded it, subverted its dreadful indifference, moralized it— until they had made a Mesopotamia in America."

His utopia-building under way, Young launched the most ambitious communal socialist society in the history of the country. He divided the nascent city into individual lots for homes, one for each family, and planned to have farms ranging in size from five to eighty acres on the outskirts of town assigned to the male Saints in accordance with the size of their families. Young decreed that there would be no private ownership of land, since it belonged to God. The harvest would be placed in communal storage for distribution according to individual need.

By 1849, when the land ceded to the United States at the end of the Mexican War had been transferred in accordance with the Treaty of Guadalupe Hidalgo, Young brashly claimed for his own free and independent empire this second-largest land acquisition in American history, a staggering mass comprising the future states of Utah and Nevada, as well as much of what would become Arizona, California, Colorado, Idaho, Wyoming, and New Mexico—an act that would not go unchallenged. For years to come, Young would wage a struggle of sovereignty with the federal government in his attempts to fulfill his dream of a nation-state.

To populate this colossal domain, he turned his sights yet again to Great Britain, dispatching his ablest men to cross the Atlantic in search of fresh converts.

What, if anything, Jean Rio Baker knew of this tumultuous history is unclear. While most missionaries were mature, married American men, it was an Englishman by the name of John

Taylor who approached the Baker family. The former Anglican had been influenced by a Scottish Presbyterian minister
in London named Edward Irving, who had attracted a large
following with his eloquent sermons on apocalyptic millenar-
ianism. This group of Irvingites consisted of upper-class intellectuals, and when Taylor abandoned the sect for Mormonism
he sought followers in the same social stratum, focusing upon
those already steeped in religious questing. Brigham Young
was brilliant at matching his missionaries to their converts—
sending farmers to recruit Scandinavians, laborers to recruit
factory workers—and he dispatched his more cerebral missionaries to cultivate the Irvingites. Raised in England's most
inspiring landscape—the Lake District, which gave inspiration to William Wordsworth and Samuel Taylor Coleridge—
Taylor rebelled against what he saw as a staid and traditional
mainstream religion. The Anglican doctrine of "sin and
unworthiness," writes one of his biographers, "didn't fit his
surging and optimistic vitality."

Drawn by the notion that regardless of "unworthiness" all
mortals could evolve into higher beings, Taylor would be one
of the earliest British converts to Mormonism. He emigrated
to Missouri shortly after his 1836 baptism. Appointed an apostle by Joseph Smith, he would accompany Smith to the
Carthage jail, where he survived being shot several times in
the melee that left the prophet dead. Taylor returned to his
native England to proselytize. A polygamist, he publicly disavowed polygamy, dismissing questions about the practice as
evilly inspired gossip. By 1848, at the time he converted the

John Taylor, an upper-class English intellectual, converted to
Mormonism in 1836. He emigrated soon afterward to Missouri,
where the founding prophet, Joseph Smith, appointed him an apostle.
He returned to England to proselytize, converting Jean Rio and
her family in 1848.

Baker family, he was the secret husband to some twelve women in Nauvoo.

The Mormon missionaries were "preaching the glory of America along with the glory of the new religion," writes Fawn Brodie, and Brigham Young was advocating emigration as a solution for Europe's social and economic problems. Taylor wrote a "memorial" to Queen Victoria, offering to remove England's poor to America through a sophisticated plan for emigration. The creation of Zion in the American New Jerusalem was "the working-class Mormon response to a class society that offered only limited opportunities for self-improvement," writes Richard L. Jensen and Malcolm R. Thorp. Most Britons who converted were attracted to the promise of relief from the economic servitude that shackled them. Guaranteed acres upon acres of soil as rich as Eden, the poor and working class clamored to leave.

For Jean Rio and those converts who were better off than the working class, the reasons were different. Her decision to join a new faith was emotional, spiritual, and intellectual. She was seduced by promises of a return to a pure, honest, original Christianity. Perhaps even more alluring to her was the Mormon message of individual salvation. Such a notion would have been liberating to a woman who had spent her life thus far subject to what she had increasingly come to see as the oppressive, intercessory role of an indifferent ecclesiastical authority.

Early missionaries pointedly neglected to reveal the doctrine of polygamy that the independent, and very monogamous, Jean Rio would later find so abhorrent. What attracted her now was the promise that women could be members of the priesthood—not, as she later learned, that a woman's only path to the hereafter was as an appendage to a man. While there had been nineteen "high priestesses" in 1843, the church had returned to a staunch patriarchy after Joseph Smith's death in 1844, but that was not disclosed to her.

She was drawn to Smith's concept that Christianity would be restored to the individual, which, after all, was the revolutionary idea that Jesus preached—that the power once held in the temple could be found within each person, that God was accessible to every human being directly rather than through the dominant male church hierarchy. "It was deeply subversive of the existing order of things," according to one religious scholar, "since it made no distinction between rich or poor, sinful or innocent, man or woman; everyone could be part of the temple on equal terms." Mormonism was a radical departure from the staid Anglican religion in which Jean Rio had been reared. Now, the missionaries assured her, she could embark on a rich and evolving personal relationship with God without a censoring male intermediary, and like all mortals, she could be guided by ongoing revelations.

Tales of Joseph Smith's martyrdom and the persecution of the Saints in Missouri strengthened her ardor. No small attraction, as well, especially for this woman whose adventuresome spirit was barely contained in London society, was the excitement of participating in the settlement of the newly explored North American continent. But such a naked desire and ambition for entering the man's world of adventure would be considered "womanly" only if cloaked in a spiritual calling. "One must be called by God or Christ to service in spiritual causes higher than one's own poor self might envision, and authorized by that spiritual call to an achievement and accomplishment in no other way excusable in a female self," writes American scholar Carolyn G. Heilbrun of this era in which it was not acceptable for women openly to seek control over their lives.

Still, a religious conversion of such magnitude was highly controversial in Jean Rio's social stratum, and was made even more so by the requisite immersion baptism gaining notoriety in the community. Based on instructions left by Joseph Smith—who said he had received a visitation from John the Baptist describing the method of complete immersion—the Mormon baptism was meant to be a literal rebirth, "according to the orders and example of our Savior, Jesus Christ," as one convert wrote. The terrifying immersions, attended as they were by rumors of fatal drownings, not surprisingly brought moments of spiritual metamorphosis to many new disciples. The clandestine baptisms were often performed at night to avoid anti-Mormon mobs, and the icy rivers and ponds held a special trepidation for the proselytes. John Taylor baptized Jean Rio Baker and her husband, Henry Baker, in London on June 18, 1849. A fellow missionary, Wilford Woodruff, baptized the Baker children around the same time. Many decades later, Taylor and Woodruff, in turn, would succeed Brigham Young as presidents and prophets of the church.

Later that summer, a cholera epidemic struck London, and Jean Rio's husband and infant daughter became gravely ill. Henry died on September 3, and the baby girl, her namesake, Jean Rio, died ten days later. The heartbroken widow turned her full attention to emigrating to America with her remaining seven children. If she agonized over this momentous decision, she did not reveal any uncertainty to the many friends and family members who attempted to dissuade her. It would have been only natural to feel misgivings about an unknown future, but her determination never failed her. If she harbored doubts, if she vacillated at all, she kept it to herself. The loss of her husband and child seemed to embolden her in her newfound purpose rather than to undermine her resolve. Only years later would she reflect on the magnitude of her decision, on all that she had left behind, ultimately judging herself harshly.

In accordance with English law, she inherited her husband's property, which added to her already sizable coffers. She set out to liquidate her holdings, converting her real property and many personal belongings to cash, and began preparations for the journey.

Millennialist predictions gave urgency to the foreign mission, as the Second Coming was said to be imminent. Jean Rio saw it all as divine intervention that would transform a corrupt and venal society into an idealistic golden age free of disease, poverty, crime, and oppression. These were what the church called the "latter days," referring to the Bible's Book of Revelation, in which it was prophesied that final wars would rage on a field called Armageddon, and floods and fires would destroy the earth. The church's mouthpiece, the *Millennial Star*, a Liverpool newspaper edited by John Taylor, carried a regular column, entitled "Signs of the Times," that interpreted the wars, volcanoes, earthquakes, plagues, fires, and floods erupting throughout the world as unmistakable portents that the end was near. Jean Rio didn't need to look far beyond the tragedy within her own family and the depravity of her community for convincing evidence.

The concept of the Mormons' gathering to Zion of the seed of Israel was the distinctive expression of the British Saints' millennialism. The renewal and evangelical impulse of Mormonism that was sweeping across England inspired untold numbers to leave behind everything familiar for the calling of a new land. With the same discipline and drive that had made her a successful musician, Jean Rio threw herself into this most passionate dedication to a richer life for herself and her children. The message of the "Restoration" was deeply felt, and the apocalypticism that infected her fellow seekers was contagious. She saw herself as fortunate to be called to participate in what she thought was one of history's most spiritual and challenging times. To join the exodus to a faraway, mysterious land as part of this calling seemed to her natural as well as epic.

While the church chartered vessels and supplied funds for the poorest converts, Jean Rio was among the few who had the means to pay their own way. This financial independence also provided her with the ability to take far more belongings than most emigrants could manage. Her square grand piano was carefully dismantled and crated, and the crate that would hold it was dipped in tar to weatherproof it for the dozens of water crossings—across the ocean, then up the Mississippi River, and finally traversing the plains, with their many streams and tributaries, en route to Utah. She packed enough stately dresses cut exclusively for her by seamstresses on London's fashionable Regent Street to wear to Sunday church services, and booked passage on a sailing ship from England to New Orleans for herself, her seven children, and nine others—friends and members of her extended family.

The British government had begun implementing regulations in response to rampant reports of overcrowded, unsanitary, criminal, and life-threatening circumstances upon the seas. By the time Jean Rio made arrangements for transportation on the newly built, 152-foot *George W. Bourne*, the law limited the payload to three passengers for every five tons, and required six feet between decks and ten square feet per passenger in lower berths. Captains were ordered to carry three quarts of fresh water per day per passenger, as well as seven pounds of bread, biscuits, flour, oatmeal, or rice per passenger per week. Ships had to be inspected for seaworthiness and had to carry a sufficient number of lifeboats.

Still, emigration took great courage. Even under the best of circumstances the perils of smallpox, measles, typhoid, lice, spoiled food, diarrhea, and common seasickness took their toll. Shipwrecks, hurricanes, collisions, leaks, and lack of wind to propel the ship at a pace in keeping with the food supply all added to the risk. The voyage ordinarily took between four and nine weeks, depending on the weather and the infamous headwinds on the Atlantic—what one historian calls "a formidable gauntlet of wind and wave." After the arrival in New Orleans, a thousand-mile riverboat excursion up the Mississippi River to St. Louis offered its own dangers. Snags, sandbars, collisions, explosions, fires, and floods threatened the steamboats. Between 1810 and 1850, more than four thousand people had died in steamboat calamities. In the American interior, disease posed a unique threat to British emigrants, who had little immunity to afflictions such as Rocky Mountain spotted fever. Families rarely arrived in Zion intact.

Crossing twelve hundred miles of plains carried hazards as well, including wagon accidents, buffalo stampedes, lightning strikes, poisonous snakes and insects, Indian depredations, sunstroke, exhaustion, theft, and noxious water. Missionaries downplayed the dangers; church leaders believed the voyage would strengthen the converts for the hardship of life in Zion. Hints of the aridity of the Salt Lake Valley made their way to England, as the Mormon elders requested certain supplies. But most emigrants would be shocked to find Zion a barren desert rather than the sylvan Eden they had been promised. Jean Rio certainly had no intention of farming, nor had she yet been told that eventually she would be expected to "consecrate" all of her money and possessions to the prophet Brigham Young. Having spent her life in the lush verdure of England, she would be unprepared for the harsh aridity and drought-ridden land of her future home.

At forty years old, she believed she had sufficient resources for the rest of her life. Her gold, diamond, and sapphire jewelry, musical instruments, personal library, printed music, bone china, sterling tableware, damask linens, and Queen Anne furniture, as well as an elegant wardrobe, suggest that she anticipated a life if not of leisure then at least of a certain comfort.

The church provided Jean Rio with detailed publications about the requisite supplies for the journey as well as for life in Zion. Since there were few stores in Utah, she was told to bring a substantial amount of clothing, linen, thread, needles and pins, and tools including a claw hammer and nails, as well as to procure some firearms, especially rifles, and ammunition. Writing paper and cooking utensils were also in short supply in Utah and had to be brought.

Leaving her husband of seventeen years and her two deceased children interred at the St. Lawrence Jewry, Jean Rio turned her attention away from her homeland and toward a new frontier. With the anguish of parting from friends and relatives, she bought passage for her seventeen-member entourage, which included her seventeen-year-old son, Henry Walter (called simply "Walter"), and his young bride, Eliza; fifteen-year-old William; eleven-year-old Charles Edward; nine-year-old Elizabeth; seven-year-old John; six-year-old Charles West, and a sickly four-year-old, Josiah. She would also pay for her brother-in-law Benjamin Baker; her husband's only sister, Mary Ann Bateman, and Mary Ann's husband, Jeremiah, who had recently lost their twin daughters to tuberculosis; and five additional converts for whom she took responsibility.

Just as her mother, Susanna Burgess, had escaped persecution in France for the promise of life in England, Jean Rio now abandoned the severity and constraints of that England for a country halfway around the world. The great Romantic notion of true freedom from all kinds of oppression was symbolized by the young nation of unlimited possibility.

Her social standing and personal wealth had been no protection against the spiritual vacuum that she felt at home. Women, regardless of their station, were not empowered by Victorian society, and the promise of the missionaries, the community of the Saints—whatever the reality would turn out to be—was the promise of more autonomy and respect than a future in England held for her. She possessed a well-defined social conscience that gave her a lifelong commitment to improving the lives of those less fortunate. Her writing and her life make clear that she was seeking a more primitive Christianity that would enhance her identification with the poor and oppressed. The attraction of Mormonism was a communal ideal that had implicit within it more of a rigorous social conscience than any other American religion of the time, and far more than the Anglican religion of early-nineteenth-century England. If she harbored any doubts, they were suppressed by her overwhelming belief that there existed a better place and a more fulfilling life for herself and her children.

CHAPTER FOUR

Committed to the Deep

I THIS DAY TOOK LEAVE of every acquaintance I could collect together, in all probability never to see them again on earth. I am now, with my children, about to leave forever my Native Land, in order to gather with the Saints of the Church of Christ, in the Valley of the Great Salt Lake in North America." This first diary entry by Jean Rio was made on January 4, 1851.

The next day, she and her party rode the train from London to the thriving English port of Liverpool. The harbor was filled with hundreds of masts bearing flags from dozens of nations on "schooners, barks, barkentines, brigs, snows, sloops, steamers, tugs, and fishing boats," as Conway B. Sonne describes the more than twenty thousand vessels that used the docks that year. There the voyagers would get the first glimpse of the ship that would carry them across the Atlantic, a 663-ton square-rigger built in Kennebunk, Maine, two years earlier. Commanded by her co-owner, Captain William Williams, the vessel was "a typical product of Yankee shipwrights, built with two decks but no galleries, three masts, square stern, and a billethead," as a maritime encyclopedia describes the ship.

The Kennebec River region was known for the finest ships built in America, and the *George W. Bourne*—the namesake of her builder—was an impressive specimen of seasoned spruce and pine fashioned into a sleek and elegant craft.

A Mormon shipping agency had chartered the vessel, paid the way for most of the 181 emigrating Saints under the direction of three elders, and provided the necessary food for the trip, though Jean Rio paid amply to transport her own family. The other converts borrowed money from the church-founded Perpetual Emigrating Fund—financed with voluntary contributions in Utah—money they were expected to repay in labor, livestock, or goods upon their arrival in Salt Lake City. "The funds are appropriated in the form of a loan, rather than a gift," Brigham Young wrote, "and this will make the honest in heart rejoice, for they love to labor, and be independent by their labor, and not live on the charity of their friends, while the lazy idlers, if any such there be, will find fault, and want every luxury furnished them for their journey, and in the end pay nothing. The Perpetual Fund will help no such idlers; we have no use for them in the Valley." The revolving cooperative fund enabled Mormons already living in Utah to make deposits in Salt Lake City to pay for transportation of their family and friends who were still in the British Isles, and in Scandinavia, where missionaries were working feverishly.

At the time, the average cost from Liverpool to what is now Council Bluffs, Iowa, where the wagon-train excursion to Zion would begin, was ten English pounds per person—approximately three times a factory worker's annual salary. In Council Bluffs, the church would outfit the teams, though, again, Jean Rio would buy her own wagons and oxen and hire teamsters, professional men who would drive her teams across the plains. She prepared herself by reading the recently published travel guides and poring over maps created by explorers and provided by the church.

On January 7 she and her children passed their required medical examinations before boarding the ship, even though four-year-old Josiah was grievously ill from consumption, from which he had been suffering throughout the previous months. Having recently lost her husband and another child to disease, she well knew the severity of his condition. Still, she hoped that the sea air would revitalize him and she knew that in any case he would never have survived the London winter.

She wore a woolen cape to keep out the damp Liverpool chill. There was no one to bid her farewell, but she felt blessed to have a sunny day for departure. She was not without her fears and worries, but her overwhelming mood was one of excitement and even levity. She found great humor in her group's allocated provision of seventy pounds of oatmeal for the first week.

The initial days were occupied with organizational tasks controlled by the church leaders. Elder William Gibson quickly established order and appointed a committee composed of himself and two other church officials. The three then divided the ship into wards, each ward to be presided over by one of them, and appointed men to act as security for the group and to keep order. Next came the reading of a strict code of conduct to be observed while at sea. The passengers received explicit instructions on hygiene and sanitation, and were warned about lascivious drunken sailors and backsliding converts.

Passengers were expected to rise at six a.m., then clean their berths and throw all garbage overboard; they were to air their bedding twice a week before morning prayer. After prayer, the passengers would return to their personal quarters—furnished by the emigrants themselves with beds and bedding and all cooking utensils—to prepare breakfast. After the meal they would spend the day writing letters, reading, and entertaining themselves. A large "supper" was served around noon, tea at three p.m., and a small meal around six p.m. At eight p.m., prayers were again offered, after which the emigrants would retire for the night.

Lectures were scheduled for the adults and classes set up for the children, with regular church services to be held on Sundays. The management and harmony of the Mormon ships were in great contrast to so many of the overcrowded, chaotic expeditions of the day, prompting Charles Dickens to note "the perfect order and propriety of all their social arrangements." Under the logistical direction of Brigham Young, the Mormon emigration became legendary for its discipline and control. The swift punishment of apostates, or dissidents, ensured that only the most tenacious, most loyal would be gathered to Zion.

On January 11 the ship was towed out into the Mersey River, where the sails were unfurled and the captain waited for a "fair wind" to carry the ship into the sea a few miles away. But the ship was stuck there for days as heavy winds blew against it, pushing it backward—"the ship rolls as badly as if she were off the North Foreland Cape in a gale," Jean Rio wrote. Then those aboard waited for the winds to shift in their favor. On January 23, at ten a.m., a tug hauled the ship out into the Irish Sea. Now, it seemed, the journey across the Atlantic would begin. But instead the passengers faced more wind "dead against us," so that nearly everyone on board was seasick. "We who have hitherto escaped are obliged to hold on to anything that comes in our way in order to keep our feet," Jean Rio wrote.

The next day the winds continued, with all but ten persons on board violently ill. "Myself, I am happy to say, with Eliza, are in the minority," wrote Jean Rio. With the ship roiling end on end, the passengers were seized with a paralyzing fear. Such fear was not unfounded, with shipwrecks and vanishing vessels all too common. "As to myself," Jean Rio wrote, "the sea has never had any terrors." But the darkness and creaking that pervaded the ship at night, the vomiting passengers and crying children, the agitated sailors and wind-whipped sails unnerved even the most resolute of souls. One young woman went into labor as the sea hurled the helpless boat. When she delivered a healthy baby boy, after the most "dreadful night," optimism was restored. The sacraments administered that Sunday brought new courage to a demoralized company.

Five days later they were in sight of the mountainous Irish coast, Dublin Bay filled with fishing boats and large ships. Finally, wrote Jean Rio, the winds had shifted, and escaping "this terrible Irish Sea" seemed imminent. She spent most of her time caring for little Josiah, who was weak but not markedly worse than at the time of their departure. Praying fervently that the sea would bring a curative miracle for the child, she alternated between attending to him and to the rest of her wretchedly seasick children and her in-laws.

On February 2, nearly a month after departure, they reached the Atlantic Ocean, traveling at a speed of eleven miles an hour. On that day Jean Rio cooked their last piece of fresh meat and burrowed in for what now seemed an interminable journey as the winds ebbed and arose again. She carried Josiah to the deck to show him the school of porpoises playing around the boat. A Dutch ship that saluted them broke the solitude of the broad expanse. But just as quickly as the wind had risen, it fell into a dead calm. "The folks at home, I suppose, are sitting by a good fire while we are on deck enjoying the view of a smooth sea in a warm sunshine," she wrote.

Captivated by the serenity, she struggled to keep her own spirits high: "I can hardly describe the beauty of this night, the moon nearly at its fullest with a deep blue sky studded with stars, the reflection of which makes the sea appear like an immense sheet of diamonds." Walking the deck late in the evening without a bonnet or a shawl, she noted the contrast of a calm sea with an earlier day when "we were shivering between decks and not able to keep our feet without holding fast to something or other. And if we managed to get on the upper deck, the first salute was a great lump of water in the face." She went on: "I have seen the mighty deep in its anger with our ship nearly on her beam ends, and I have seen it, as now, under a cloudless sky and scarcely a ripple on its surface, and I know not which to admire most. I cannot describe it as it ought to be described, but I feel most powerfully the force of these words: 'the Mighty God,' which Handel has so beautifully expressed in one of his chronicles."

On February 15, at the sign of "squally weather," Josiah took a turn for the worse. As the winds became violent, Jean Rio joined her family for supper on the deck, where they were barely able to hold on to their plates as "shoals of flying fish" erupted before them. Then, as the ship pitched against the waves, six-year-old Charles West fell down the hatchway, landing on his head. His injuries were so serious that Jean Rio feared he might die, and his disorientation was made worse by a seeping eye inflammation that sealed his eyelids shut.

A week later Charles was still suffering, but it was her youngest who had sunk rapidly into death. At five-thirty p.m. on February 22, "my very dear little Josiah breathed his last." Jean Rio felt that God had intervened to end her child's suffering. She beseeched the captain to let her "retain his little body until tomorrow, when it will be committed to the deep nearly a thousand miles from land, there to remain until the word goes forth for the sea to give up its dead."

Devastated by the loss, she faltered briefly in her stoicism. She was shaken by the reality that she would not be able to take her family "safely through to the city in the tops of the mountains," in a reference to the Biblical Isaiah: "Now it shall come to pass in the latter days, that the mountain of the Lord's house shall be established in the tops of the mountains, and shall be exalted above the hills; and all nations shall flow to it." The child's body was removed to a cabin under the forecastle, where the older males of her family kept vigil over it throughout the night.

Jean Rio arose at dawn the next morning, a bright and clear Sunday she described as "beautiful." Her brother-in-law Jeremiah and the ship's second mate sewed "the body of our dear little fellow ready for burial," encasing the boy in a canvas shroud. Attached to his feet was a mass of coal sufficient to sink the shroud to the bottom of the ocean.

At eleven o'clock, Jean Rio heard the tolling of the ship's bell announcing the time had come. With her pen, she noted in her diary that the ship was at "44/14 west longitude, 25/13 north latitude." She then went on deck for the burial of her last-born son. "This is my first severe trial after leaving my native land," she wrote. "But the Lord has answered my prayer in this one thing: that if it was not His will to spare my boy to reach his destined home with us, that He would take him while we were on the sea. For I would much rather leave his body in the ocean than bury him in a strange land and leave him there."

As quickly as the calm had appeared, the sea turned tempestuous again. Jean Rio awakened the following morning to a dense fog enveloping the ship and a torrential rainstorm that dropped four inches of water in five minutes. The crew scrambled to bring in the sails and ordered all passengers below deck. For an hour the ship rolled against the waves.

By the next day Charles was able to open his eyes into tiny slits, and the bandages on his head were removed. Without meat for nearly a month, some of the Mormon men decided to kill one of the porpoises swimming alongside the ship. They struck a five-foot-long dolphin with a plank and hauled it on board. After it was skinned and cut into servings, one of them presented Jean Rio with a piece. But she was unable to eat it, finding its coarseness and dark color unappealing.

For days, storms and hot weather dogged the ship. The sea was covered with foam and gulfweed. Only the vision of flying fish and the ever-changing sky broke the monotony. "Our ship is the center of an immense circle, bounded only by the clouds," Jean Rio wrote. "All is grand and beautiful and fully repays me for the inconvenience of a sea voyage." Now, nearly six weeks at sea, the passengers had settled into a routine and life proceeded in its ordinariness: a baby was born, couples were married, disputes arose and were mediated. A bugle sounded at six o'clock every morning, and after breakfast, prayer, and the required chores were completed, the converts broke into small groups to play music or "gossip so the days pass along." They had all acquired what the sailors called their sea legs, and Jean Rio prided herself in being able to "walk about the ship" regardless of the weather. She began to take pleasure in the mercurial swells she called "awful, yet grand." In her diary she compared the waves to "the boiling of an immense kettle, covered with white foam, while the roaring of the winds and waves was like the bellowing of a thousand wild bulls."

Though many on board were terrified, she remained daunt-less. The only inconvenience, she noted, was the aching in her bones from the "incessant motion." The fact that the head-winds had driven them back hundreds of miles broke the spirit of many, but she relished the entire adventure: "I could only look, wonder and admire, for through all our literal ups and downs I have felt no fear."

The collective mood improved on March 9, as the ship passed the Bahamas and the expectation of their soon reaching America grew. The harsh winds shifted to cool breezes, and the cerulean hues of the Caribbean had a tranquilizing effect on the company, whose nerves had been especially frayed after the excommunication of one of their elders for "inconsistent conduct." Elder William Booth, who had conducted the funeral service for little Josiah, had had sexual relations with Sister Thorn, the wife of a fellow elder, and this "deeply grieved" her husband and shocked the Saints who had entrusted their spiritual salvation to this man. "We all hope he will soon be able to forget her entirely," Jean Rio wrote of the aggrieved Elder Thorn. Then, three of the more respected women in the company were excommunicated for "levity of behavior with some of the officers of the ship."

Now the Caribbean torridity blasted the passengers, with "nearly half of our company affected more or less with the prickly heat." The ship's captain provided a large tub of fresh water for "dipping" the children, who were covered from head to toe with an irritating rash. "The men amuse themselves after another fashion," Jean Rio wrote. "They put on a thin pair of drawers and pour buckets of water over each other."

On the evening of March 10 they caught their first glimpse of a stationary, revolving light. Passing within three miles of what Jean Rio identified as the Island of Great and Little Isaacs and Green Turtle Island—now-defunct names for islands off the coast of Cuba—they celebrated the first sight of civilization they had had in nearly ten weeks. The lighthouse was situated on an island forty miles long, an uninhabited stretch except for a harbor where dozens of small schooners were anchored.

"Passed Buch Island, also Double-Headed Shot," Jean Rio wrote in her diary on March 12. "This is not exactly an island but a long chain of rocks." The ship entered the Gulf of Mexico two days later, and from that point forward the climate was "immensely hot." She counted seventeen sailboats of various sizes, elegant against the aquamarine bay. "I have often wondered and read of the beauty of Italian skies, but I am sure they cannot exceed in splendor that which, at this moment, arches over the Gulf of Florida, or Mexico, as it is mostly determined."

The next day, the crew measured the fresh water on board the ship and calculated that there remained a twenty-three-day supply. Despite the delays on the open sea, the company was well supplied, and there was ample water for the final jaunt across the gulf to New Orleans. Jean Rio was taken with the scenery and the fact that they had almost arrived, and she refused to succumb to the pessimism and apprehension infecting many on board. "At seven in the evening a violent squall came on," she wrote, "driving most of the passengers below. Myself, with a few others, remained on deck, bidding defiance to the rain for the sake of enjoying the night of lightning which was very beautiful, seeming to illuminate one half of the horizon at once." Even though the night was as rough as "when skirting the Bay of Biscay," she stayed up to watch the light show. When the rest of her family fell prey to seasickness, she remained absorbed in the momentous occasion. "To my astonishment," she wrote upon awakening the following morning, "the sun was rising on our starboard now," and the water was "a perfect mirror."

At noon on March 18, a steamship came out to meet the boat and pull it in to anchor at the island of Belize. "A boat has come alongside us loaded with oysters, which have found a ready market," she wrote. The houses in the village were reflected perfectly in the water. "There is a small schooner lying at anchor just by the landing place, and every rope and block in her rigging is seen reversed exactly as if standing on an immense looking glass."

The next morning a steamer took the *George W. Bourne* in tow, pulling the battered but intact vessel 110 miles up the Mississippi River to New Orleans. "America at last!" Jean Rio wrote upon arrival in the city two days later.

> To describe the scenery on each side of this mighty stream needs a better pen than mine. No description that I have ever read has done it anything like justice. Sugar and cotton plantations abound. The houses of the planters are built in cottage style, but large, with verandas on every side and beautiful gardens. At a little distance are the Negro huts, from thirty to fifty on each plantation. They are built of wood with a veranda along the front, painted white. And most have either jasmine or honeysuckle growing over them. Each cottage has a long piece of garden ground attached to it. In general appearance they are certainly very far superior to the cottages inhabited by the poor in England. Groves of orange trees are very numerous, the perfume from which is very

delightful as the breeze wafts it toward us. Thousands of peach and plum trees are here growing wild and are now in full blossom. We saw plenty of wild geese, also foxes and a raccoon or two. Storks fly here in numbers, over our heads, and settle down on the riverside and stretch out their long necks, looking at us as if in astonishment. There is an endless variety of landscape. The only thing that detracts from its beauty is the sign of the hundreds of Negroes at work in the sun. Oh, slavery, how I hate thee!

Fifty-six days after clearing the Liverpool harbor, on March 20, 1851, the ship had reached America. Elder Gibson proudly wrote in his official report that no company of Saints had ever crossed the Atlantic with fewer catastrophes: "This pleasant voyage was marked by one marriage, three births, two converts among crew members, and the death of a small boy who was dying of consumption when he boarded the ship."

Church officials cautioned the emigrants about swindlers who used what one writer described as "ardent spirits" to lower the Saints' guard, and especially about the rich French cuisine that could wreak havoc on the stomachs of those who had subsisted for almost two months on little more than biscuits and oatmeal.

Eager to disembark, Jean Rio would spend the next two days at an opulent residence in the "Paris of the Bayous"—at that time the world's fourth-ranking port, second only to New York City in the United States, and one of the wealthiest cities in the country. She carried a letter of introduction from her friend "Miss Longhurst of Grover Street, Bedford Square" to

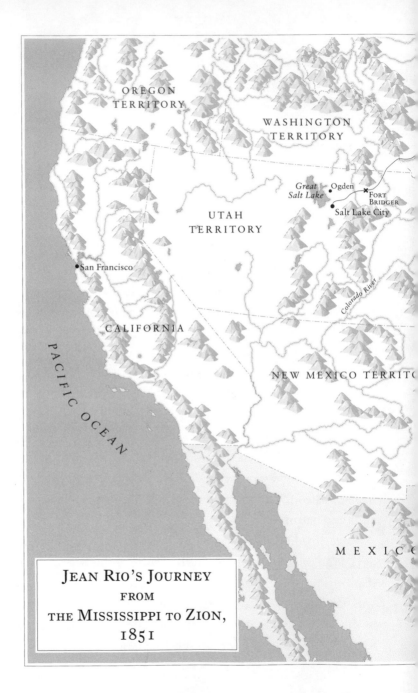

OREGON
TERRITORY

WASHINGTON
TERRITORY

*Great
Salt Lake* •Ogden
✕ FORT
BRIDGER
•Salt Lake City

UTAH
TERRITORY

•San Francisco

Colorado River

CALIFORNIA

PACIFIC OCEAN

NEW MEXICO TERRITO

MEXICO

JEAN RIO'S JOURNEY
FROM
THE MISSISSIPPI TO ZION,
1851

Miss Longhurst's sister, Mrs. Blime, "the wife of a French gentleman residing here." Bursting into tears at the sight of a
countrywoman, Mrs. Blime gave Jean Rio a guided tour in a
horse-drawn carriage through the wide but unpaved city
streets.

"The roads themselves are not kept in order as they are in
London," Jean Rio wrote. "Just now the weather is hot and dry,
so in crossing them you sink in dust up to the ankles. In wet
seasons, I am told, they are one continuous canal. Great lumps
of stone are placed across the ends of the streets, about two
feet under, to enable foot passengers to go from one side to
another." It was the first time she had seen a city laid out in
"exact squares, crossing each other at right angles. The spaces
between the streets are called blocks."

The flavor and culture of the city was unmistakably
French, though the population seemed evenly split between
the French and the "Negroes." Never before in all her world
travels had she seen a city so conspicuously divided between
the rich and the poor. Palatial estates lined Bourbon and Royal
streets, while the ubiquitous ramshackle slave quarters dotted
the outlying areas. She was particularly taken with the attire of
both the haves and the have-nots.

> The higher class of citizens—there is no nobility in America,
> though never was there a people fonder of titles: colonels,
> majors, captains, judges, and squires being as plentiful as
> blackberries—the Upper-Ten dress very handsomely in
> European style, the ladies especially, and they dress their
> slaves even more expensively. I saw slave girls following their

mistresses in the streets, clad in frocks of embroidered silk or satin, and elegantly worked muslin trousers, either blue or scarlet, Morocco walking shoes and white silk stockings, with a French headdress similar to that worn by the Savoyards, composed of silk with all the colors of the rainbow co-mingled. Jewelry glitters on their dusky fingers (which are plainly seen through their lace gloves) and in their ears. Their only business in the streets seems to be to follow the ladies who own them and carry their reticule.

Bonnets are not worn, but a queer-looking thing made of muslin, something like the Quakers' bonnets except that the front is not rounded off. They are stiffened with cane or strips of pasteboard. The front is twelve inches deep, with a horseshoe crown, and curtain half a yard in depth, and when on the head answers the purpose of bonnet and shawl. I thought them the most odd-looking things I had seen, but was soon glad to avail myself of the comfort of one in this blazing sun.

Mrs. Blime provided her with sumptuous guest quarters, and Jean Rio, accustomed as she was to a lavish lifestyle, was stupefied by the opulence. "For breakfast they take coffee boiled in milk," she wrote,

with eggs, ham, hung beef, dried fish, salads, hot soda cakes, bread and butter. For dinner we had boiled redfish, stewed pigs' feet, rumsteaks, wild goose (rabbits and squirrels too are commonly eaten) with vegetables, pickles, and salad. Two tumblers are put to each plate, and wine and brandy are placed on the table and each takes which they please. The idea of pouring either in wine glasses they laugh at—even ladies will drink off a tumbler of port as if it was water. Pies, tarts, cheesecakes, candy, fruit, and ice cream are brought on table after the meats are removed. French brandy poured into a glass and most bountifully sweetened with pulverized sugar finishes the meal. Tea as a meal they know nothing about, but at seven o'clock they take supper, which is quite as luxurious an affair as the dinner. By ten o'clock everyone is in bed and the streets are deserted.

Her hostess explained that while most of New Orleans's white inhabitants were Frenchmen, they were nearly all married to Englishwomen, and she suggested that Jean Rio could fashion a nice life for herself there rather than continuing on to this mysterious Zion. If Jean Rio entertained the notion at all, her extant diary does not reflect it.

Desirous to oblige her guest, Mrs. Blime agreed to Jean Rio's wish to visit a slave market, and early the next morning arranged to attend the auction held in the city's Customs House. Women were prohibited from entering the "slave market for males," so Jean Rio satisfied herself with that for women.

It is a large hall, well lighted, with seats all around on which were girls of every shade of color, from ten or twelve to thirty years of age. To my utter astonishment they were singing as merrily as larks. I expressed my surprise to Mrs. Blime. "Ah," she said, "though I as an Englishwoman detest the very idea of slavery, yet I do believe that many of the slaves here have ten times the comforts of the laborers in our own country, with not half the labor. I have been thirteen years in this country, and although I have never owned a slave or ever intend to do so, still I do not look upon slavery with the horror that I once did. There are hundreds of slaves here who would not accept their freedom if it was offered to them. For this reason: they would then have no protection, as the laws afford little or none to people of color." I could not help thinking that my friend's feelings had become somewhat blunted, if not hardened, by long residence in a slave state.

They returned to the Blime estate and engaged in a lively dialogue on the issue. Jean Rio learned that the conditions for slaves had changed dramatically since the Louisiana Purchase in 1803, and that African slaves had received far better treatment when New Orleans was a French colony than after the Americans took control. Jean Rio was confounded by the nuances. "From further conversation," she wrote in her diary that night,

I found that if a free man marries a slave, all the children of that marriage are the property of the owner of the mother. But if a free woman marries a slave, the children are free. I was shown a gentleman of color who is what we should call "managing clerk" in one of the largest stores in this city. He is the property of a rich proprietor in the neighborhood. He pays his master $500 annually and his salary is $1,000. He is married to a free woman, quite a light mulatto, by whom he has a family. They live in a very handsome house, which is the property of the wife, as a slave is not allowed to possess real estate. They keep a carriage and four servants, and this is by no means a singular case. It is a common occurrence for masters to hire out their slaves in this way at a salary of from fifty to seventy dollars per month, out of which they pay their masters an agreed-upon sum. The rest is their own.

Struggling to understand an arrangement clearly more complex than she had gathered from the British literature on the subject, she remained unconvinced of its benign aspects as presented by her hostess. "In spite of all of this," she wrote of the apologia, "the system is a horrible one to English minds. Well might Sterne [an apparent reference to Laurence Sterne, the English clergyman and author of *The Life and Opinions of Tristram Shandy, Gentleman*] say, 'Oh, Slavery, disguise thyself as thou wilt, thou art a bitter drought.' " Like many of her British compatriots, Jean Rio thought slavery a crime against humanity as well as a sin against God—a cruel and antiquated system that had been abolished throughout the British dominions nearly twenty years earlier.

With melancholy, she left Mrs. Blime to join her family still ensconced on the anchored *George W. Bourne.* "I should have greatly preferred spending a few more days with this truly amiable, generous lady and her family," she wrote. Loaded with "presents consisting of the delicacies of the climate accompanied with several bottles of French brandy and claret," she returned to the ship that had been her home since January. "We agreed on, and separated with, I believe, a mutual feeling that we should meet no more on earth." Such partings were now taken in stride, so accustomed had Jean Rio become to the string of good-byes in her life. But years later she would remember her brief stay in New Orleans with a wistful curiosity. What if she had stayed?

CHAPTER FIVE

Snags and Sawyers

O N MARCH 23, 1851, the steamboat *Concordia* pulled alongside the ship and the Saints' trunks and other luggage were transferred to the boat that would carry Jean Rio's party 1,250 miles up the Mississippi to St. Louis, Missouri. It would take four men to carry the piano up the ramp, and, as always when the instrument was transported, Jean Rio watched with concern. All the other passengers from the ocean crossing—including the five converts for whom Jean Rio had bought passage—had left New Orleans immediately upon their arrival, not having the resources to sightsee there. They were en route to a Mormon way station in Alexandria, Missouri, a base camp for setting out for Council Bluffs. Now, after Josiah's death at sea, Jean Rio's group numbered eleven—she and her six children, her son Henry's young wife, and her three in-laws on her husband's side.

The 499-ton side-wheel paddleboat had been built in Cincinnati four years earlier and was commanded by Captain William Cable. Jean Rio made a point of befriending the captain, from whom she was determined to glean all the necessary and useful information for the forthcoming journey. The flat-bottomed wooden vessel had its engines and boilers on the deck. The "firemen who have an uninterrupted view of the country" constantly stoked open holes on either side with fuel. Descending to the "hurricane" deck, she came upon a five-foot-wide open gallery filled with chairs to accommodate the passengers. A low railing barely above the water's edge surrounded this deck. "On the inner side of the gallery is a row of cabins," she wrote, "with two doors each—one opening onto the gallery, the other into the saloon, which is 150 feet in length by 30 feet in width." The ladies' cabin was separate, and "splendidly furnished with sofas, rocking chairs, work tables, and a piano. The floor, as well as the saloon's, is covered with Brussels carpeting." There was also "a smoking room for the gentlemen," equipped with numerous card tables for gambling. A contemporary of Jean Rio's, the English artist Frederick Hawkins Piercy, described the steamers as "floating palaces, open to, and for the use of, all who can pay, negroes excepted." Piercy continued, "A colored man, however well educated or wealthy, dare not show his nose in the saloon, he must confine himself to the deck, with the deck hands."

A staircase ascended to the upper deck, where the officers' cabins and the pilothouse were located. "The one forward encloses the steering wheel. Here stands the pilot completely secluded from the wind and weather," wrote Jean Rio. The pilot communicated with the engineers and laborers below by means of bell signals.

The captain explained the mechanism of the ship to Jean Rio, showing her two ropes attached to the wheel and then to a lever that moved the rudder. "The whole arrangement is very simple and the elevated position of the pilot, forty feet above the lower deck, enables him to see and avoid the collision with snags, which are plentiful still though the government has done much toward clearing them away," she wrote. Snag boats routinely patrolled the river, sending divers down to cut the debris from the river bottom. Like icebergs in the ocean, the "snags and sawyers" posed a great risk to the steamboats. "A snag is a large tree which has either been uprooted by a hurricane or loosened by an inundation, and at last been blown into the river." The heaviest part of the tree sinks to the bottom and becomes fixed in the mud in an upright position. As the foliage decays the naked trunk remains above the surface of the water. A sawyer is far more dangerous, she learned, for it is the same as a snag except that the top of the tree remains invisible below the surface. Steamboats hitting a sawyer could sink within minutes.

"I have run away from the upper deck, which is not a very pleasant place except in cloudy weather . . . although on a moonlit night the view is delightful, at least to such an admirer of wild scenery as I." In a headwind, the upper deck was covered with hot cinders. "They burn wood, not coal, and when the steam gets low or they want to pass a steamer in advance of them, the firemen throw on resin by shovelfuls." As an official mail carrier, the *Concordia* was the fastest boat on the river, gliding past enormous sugar plantations and tropical groves on both shores.

Within five days Jean Rio and her company had arrived in St. Louis. She was fortunate to have the financial wherewithal that allowed her to linger and truly observe a part of her new country, as she had done in New Orleans. Now she was determined to experience St. Louis, the exciting frontier outfitting post for all of the expeditions heading west in the expansionist fever of the moment. Besides which, she knew her group would be more comfortable ensconced in a home in St. Louis than sleeping on the ground at the overcrowded base camp. She calculated the time it would take her to rendezvous with the Saints at Council Bluffs before they began their long wagon-train journey to Utah, and then rented a large house, where she intended to remain for several weeks. She hired a team of men to bring her party's numerous personal effects there, including the unwieldy crated piano.

With two parlors, two bedrooms, and an outhouse "answering all the purposes of kitchen and washhouse," the temporary residence was a welcome respite after the months on the water. "The next discovery I made," Jean Rio wrote, "was that I wanted a cooking stove, which I purchased with all the utensils belonging for fourteen dollars." Her children immediately scouted the neighborhood for playmates, enjoying themselves "finely in their rambles about the town and the open country beyond." She stocked her kitchen from the many markets that opened at four a.m. every day. "All kinds of meat, poultry, and fish are very cheap. The fresh meat is good, but not so large and fat as in the English markets. Vegetables and fruit are abundant and of great variety."

She was amazed by the ever-changing weather. "This, I am told, is the general character of American springtime." On one day there could be a heavy fall of snow and freezing temperatures necessitating fires in all the fireplaces, and the very next day she would "throw open the windows."

Of particular interest to her in bustling St. Louis were the dozens of churches of every denomination, all "magnificent buildings" and all sporting steeples. "The Catholics have three churches, each surmounted with a large gilded cross, the Presbyterians three, the Baptists four, the Episcopalians and Independents several each," she noted. Then there are the Methodist and Lutheran and Swedish churches, so that religions are as plentiful as can be wished. The poor sons of Africa, too, have a little church to pray and praise the Lord in, but it is only lately that their masters have allowed them this privilege." She attended several services, primarily to hear the music, and found the orchestral bands and tenor soloists up to professional standards.

On Palm Sunday she went to Mass at a Catholic church, marveling at the rich velvet and satin coverings of the altar and at the carved walnut rails polished to a deep sheen. "On each side are seats for the scholars and Nuns of the adjoining convents. Strange-looking beings, these last. They wear black woolen shawls reaching down to the hem of their coarse black Camelot gowns, a close bonnet made of black glazed cambric, and black crepe veils reaching to the knees." The priests too donned long black gowns with a hemp cord around the waist upon which hung a rosary and crucifix. The vestments, customs, tapers, incense, Latin hymns, confessional boxes, holy water, and religious icons were foreign to her; they had been absent from the Church of England since the Protestant Reformation. She found the confessionals gloomy and mysterious, cloaked with dark green curtains and ornamented with "finely executed oil paintings but horrible to look at, being all of them representations of the martyrdom of different Saints."

Over the next two or three weeks she reviewed the list of required provisions itemized by Mormon leaders, and set out to acquire them. She purchased four wagons and eight yoke of young oxen, or sixteen animals, for the wagon-train journey across the plains, a steer for beef, and two dairy cows so that her children would have fresh milk and cheese along the way. The church list included one thousand pounds of flour, a musket or rifle for each male over the age of twelve, one pound of gunpowder, four pounds of lead, one pound of tea, five pounds of coffee, one hundred pounds of sugar, ten pounds of rice, numerous spices, cooking utensils, tents for sleeping, furnishings for the wagons, twenty-five pounds of salt, thirty pounds of dried apples and peaches, twenty-five pounds of grain, twenty pounds of soap, fifteen pounds of iron and steel, pulleys and ropes for river crossings, farming and mechanical tools, fishhooks and line for all in the party, and sundry additional items. One of the wagons was specially built to carry her square grand piano and delicate finery, the wagon itself covered with tar to protect it from the rain and dirt.

She then bought passage on yet another steamboat, the *Financier,* which would take her and her family, along with her wagons, livestock, and supplies, up the Mississippi to Alexandria. From there they would travel overland across Iowa to meet the company of Saints who would join them on the trek to the Salt Lake Valley. Two barges were attached to the steamboat, one for the cattle and one for the wagons. Waiving their rights to berths on board, Jean Rio and her family members decided they should make their beds in the wagons instead of trying to sleep with the constant jerking "always caused by the action of machinery."

When she awoke in the morning and drew aside the curtain at the front of her wagon, she found herself facing an immense wall of rock hundreds of feet in height and topped with lush greenery. "I cannot describe the grandeur of the scenery; it was almost appalling," she wrote. "In some places it seemed as if the pressure of a finger would have sent it toppling down; the rocky shores are so perpendicular that our boat could safely run in close enough for us to pluck the blossoms off the trees which grow at their base and in the crevices." Every few miles they would come to a town built on the riverbank. In between the settlements were small farms of approximately sixty acres, with cattle, sheep, and pigs grazing in the fields and chickens running free. "The man and his elder children would in most cases look at us as we passed, sometimes waving their hands to us by way of a salute, while the wife would stand at the door, mostly with a child in her arms. We passed hundreds of these farms."

That afternoon an inebriated passenger walked past Jean Rio and fell overboard into the river. The boat stopped, and every effort was made to save him. As the man struggled, he threw his wallet onto the deck. Soon afterward he drowned. In the wallet was the man's address in Hannibal, Missouri, along with $275 he had earned from transporting produce from Missouri to New Orleans. The captain, who retrieved the wallet, assured Jean Rio that the money would be "restored to the relatives of the deceased."

The incident cast a pall over Jean Rio for the remainder of the trip, and she felt glad when the boat arrived in Alexandria on the evening of April 18. "A bad landing it was for our poor cattle, for the brutality of the men belonging to the boat was most shameful, and many of the poor beasts suffered much in consequence." It seemed to take forever to unload, and she felt it a small miracle that all their luggage had arrived intact.

The men in her party—her oldest sons and her brothers-in-law—learned the art of teaming, yoking the recalcitrant oxen to the wagons. None had ever worked with such animals, and their nervousness was communicated to the balky, wide-horned livestock. When the men had managed to corral the unruly oxen and harness them to the wagons, the small company of what the locals called "greenhorns" drove the animals to a nearby open space of ground in Missouri, situated directly across the river from Warsaw, Illinois. Here, four months after leaving England, they made their first encampment. They gathered firewood, which was plentiful in the area, put their kettles on, and "sat down to a comfortable cup of tea." The men then took the cattle to a large enclosure and fed them hay they had purchased upon disembarking from the *Financier*. With the help of her daughter-in-law, Eliza, and sister-in-law Mary Ann, Jean Rio made up beds in the wagons for the night. By now, the "quickening" that signaled early pregnancy for Eliza—swollen breasts and morning nausea—had turned to "showing," and the prospect of a first grandchild being born in Zion increased Jean Rio's hopes and expectations. When the men returned from the corral, the small group formed a circle and, Jean Rio wrote, "offered up our thanksgiving to the God of Heaven for bringing us here in safety through unseen and unknown dangers." They all sensed that the real adventure was only beginning.

The trials of the Mississippi River behind her, Jean Rio sat down with a lantern to write of this "Father of Waters," as the Indians named it. "I have traveled in this river 1,630 miles and I will say that so much splendid scenery, both wild and beautiful, I never expected to look upon." Now, on the eve of the overland journey, she became pensive. She did not anticipate much pleasure in the days, weeks, months, even years ahead. "We must expect a life of toil, fatigue, and many privations to which we are unaccustomed. Still, when I call to mind the various scenes through which we have passed and the thousands of miles we have traveled . . . and the manifold instances of preserving mercy we have received at the hands of our Heavenly Father, I doubt not that I shall still, if I remain faithful, enjoy the same protection upon the land as I have upon the waters."

Jean Rio could not have come to this point, could not have endured the trials already encountered and anticipated the challenges ahead, without wondering if she had made the right choice. For the first time since her conversion by the persuasive missionaries who depicted Zion as a golden Promised Land, and the Saints as God's chosen people to whom no harm could come, the reality of the situation began to haunt her thoughts. She had had stark evidence that prayer alone could not guarantee the safety of her children. Could she bear to lose another child to the myriad dangers that loomed, life-threatening hazards that made London life seem sheltered by comparison? There was nothing to do now but forge ahead, to reach within to the deepest core of her being and renew the faith in God that had been unshakable just a few months earlier. In the upcoming years she would return to that inner well many times, redefining faith itself and especially the notion of the "Kingdom of God upon Earth." But for now she would brace herself for what increasingly seemed an amorphous and uncertain future, determined to keep an open mind. "As you are aware I am not one to go through the world with my eyes shut," she wrote, as if to a friend, with as much lightheartedness as she could muster at the moment. "I expect to be able to send you some little description of my travels by land, to amuse you in a winter's evening."

Venturing into Alexandria, Jean Rio found a thriving incorporated community of a thousand souls that boasted of having a mayor, a courthouse, and a schoolhouse that did double duty as a chapel on Sundays. At a small levee was moored a "worn-out steamboat" that served as a hotel for the "Gents of the town who are fond of gambling and drinking." There she would make purchases for the venture ahead. Taking their "first lessons in oxen driving," her sons moved their little train of four wagons a mile out of town so the animals could graze. It became clear that two of the oxen that had seemed relatively healthy had in fact been abused by the boatmen beyond usefulness. Jean Rio needed to return to Alexandria to purchase two to replace them, "thus losing $46 to begin with." Yet another of the animals had been so injured that it was "doubtful whether it will recover or not."

A billowing canvas roof reminiscent of the *George W. Bourne*'s wind-filled sails covered each of her wagons. Inside pockets carried the smaller items that would be needed on the trail, so that they could easily be reached at the end of every day. Larger items—chairs, tables, cookstoves, sewing machines, desks—were crammed into the main part of the wagon, with care taken to lodge them efficiently so they wouldn't slide around with the wagon's movement.

Once the new team was in shape, Jean Rio's family party moved four miles west and encamped in a wide, grassy meadow along a branch of the Des Moines River. There they had intended to stay for a week "in order that the cattle may recover as they are in far worse condition than they were when we left St. Louis, thanks to the steamboat men," but they decided to start the trek west sooner. When the sickly animal died, Jean Rio purchased another for twenty-six dollars. She was beginning to be alarmed at the rate at which she was tapping her resources.

The inhabitants of a nearby farmhouse sold her a "plentiful supply of butter at ten cents a pound and milk at ten cents a bucketful." Her sons hunted in the nearby woods, and to her surprise they returned with a squirrel and a game bird for dinner. She found the lovely weather reminiscent of days spent in Epping Forest. Locals from the area, eager to provide useful information about the trail ahead, visited them. "Some of them appear to be intelligent and some of them exceedingly cultivated," she wrote. "One man congratulated me on having been able to escape from such a land of slavery and oppression as he said he understood England to be. I felt my British blood rising at his insulting speech, but the poor mortal evidently knew no better, so I only smiled in reply." One man brought a freshly caught twenty-five-pound catfish, which she purchased from him for a quarter.

On April 21 Jean Rio's family group joined another group that was also camping at Alexandria before joining up with the Mormons in Council Bluffs, and the next day the small train made up of some thirty people and a dozen wagons headed out together. Every day they traveled a few miles, stopping well before sunset to set up camp and retire to their wagons before the night chill came on. The road west was not a road at all, she wrote, but "a perfect succession of hills, valleys, bogs, mud holes, log bridges, quagmires, with stumps of trees a foot above the surface of the watery mud so that without the utmost care the wagons would be overturned ten times a day." She pined for the old roads of England, each day hoping the next would be better. But instead, "the changes have only been from bad to worse." Even by late May, snow fell nearly every night.

Now pushing hard, traversing the prairie of southern Iowa, even traveling on a Sunday, they began to fear they would arrive too late to meet the rest of their company at Council Bluffs. One morning one of her teams turned "sulky" and no amount of prodding and whipping could move it forward. "The teamster should drive with the team to the right," wrote the English artist Frederick Hawkins Piercy in an illustrated travel book published in 1855. "When he cries 'Gee,' the team should go from him, and when 'Haw,' come towards him. When the teamster cries 'Haw,' it is usual with a lazy team to let them feel the whip over their necks, and when 'Gee,' over their backs." But as suddenly as her oxen had balked they took off running at full speed, breaking the tongue off the wagon. "Heartsick" at the thought of returning to Alexandria to purchase a new wagon, Jean Rio was pleasantly surprised when her brother-in-law, the genteel Englishman Jeremiah Bateman, rose to the occasion. Lashing the oxen to the wagon with a piece of cord, he fashioned a repair, and the team was able to move forward. Now it was clear to all of them that from this point on they must find reserves within themselves to meet the hardships ahead, find a resourcefulness they perhaps had never known was there.

The trail seemed to become more rugged with every mile, washed out under deep puddles of water every few hundred feet. "We managed to get along until noon," she wrote, "when we halted for an hour to feed the cattle and ourselves. On looking among our company I found that there was scarcely a wagon that had not received some injury or met with some disaster or other." After eating, they set off to cross a vast prairie. "We have had to double team and so help each other out of our muddy difficulties." Soon another of her wagons was stuck, the tongue pin breaking with a jerk. It was decided they should halt for the night, since so many wagons had either sunk or been overturned.

She was constantly struck by the friendliness of the locals, who routinely offered food, assistance, and tales of the frontier. That evening, a local farmer accompanied by a "tall-looking Negro" approached their camp and offered to help repair the wagon. Two hours later the wagon was fixed, the men refused "all recompense," and two of her sons accompanied the white man back to his farm to get corn to feed their worn-out cattle. "Our black visitor remained with us and shared our supper, which consisted of coffee, bread and butter, and remains of two fine geese, which I had purchased yesterday for twenty-five cents each."

"John" entertained her with stories of the Indian war twelve years earlier in which he had participated in taking as prisoner the Sauk tribal leader Keokuk and one of his warriors. John and others had transported the two to St. Louis, where "almost all the city" came to see them on display. John "spoke of the dignity of his (Keokuk's) whole bearing and the splendid blanket and leggings he wore." When a peace was concluded, the white men presented Keokuk with "a valuable rifle, plenty of ammunition, a horse, trappings of the most expensive kind, and liberty to return to his own nation and tribe."

Fascinated, Jean Rio stayed up conversing with the man until midnight. She wrote of her "surprise at finding so much intelligence and I may add refinement, in the language and manners of our late visitor." When her son returned with the livestock feed, he told his mother he had learned from the farmer that John had been a slave since birth, but was now "free in everything but the name [he was still legally considered a slave]. He had a large farm to manage out here on the prairie, he bought and sold how he pleased, and went out and came home when he thought proper."

After everyone else retired she stayed awake for several hours longer, sitting in silence broken only by croaking frogs.

"Near us the stars glittering in the heavens and the moon shining brightly are enabling us to see for miles around us," she
wrote. "I felt at that moment a sense of security and freedom I
cannot describe."

The next day's travel was uneventful, but as the day wound
down the vista of a "continuance" of "tremendous hills" lay
before them: "As we got to the top of one, we discovered three
others, each towering above the rest." It would be but the
beginning of increasingly rugged terrain. Ascending the hills
was like "going up a flash of lightning edgeways." But the
mountains disappeared as abruptly as they had risen, and the
following day they found themselves on wide, flat prairie
again. Passing a small farmhouse with a tidy garden near the
roadside, Jean Rio and Eliza went to the door in the hope of
acquiring some fresh vegetables. What they found was an Englishwoman from their own neighborhood in London who
had been in America for seven years. The woman "rejoiced as
though she had met some of her own family."

Continuing on, their party came to a village called Dog-
town consisting of some thirty houses, a post office, and a
"doctor's shop." The road ahead would take them through a
series of small towns, through beautiful weather and gentle
forests. When one of her oxen became very sick, Jean Rio
decided to camp near the Sac-and-Fox River. A young couple
living in a farmhouse nearby invited the emigrants over, the
settlers apparently as eager to converse with them as the emigrants were to find company on the lonely trail.

Stringtown, as the next settlement was called, comprised
forty houses and stores; linen drapery, stationery, glass and

earthenware, saddles, groceries, boots, shoes, powder, and lead could be bought there. "The barroom or whiskey shop and the school house [also] does duty for church on Sundays."

Jean Rio was overwhelmed by the kindness of strangers: "Many a time when our wagons have been in the mud hole, men working in the fields have left their plows to come and help us out. Men who in our country would be called 'gentlemen' owning 500 to 1,000 acres of land. But it seems to be a rule among them to help everyone who is in need. And they are ready at all times to impart any information which they think will be useful to us." The frontier wives were just as hospitable, generously supplying the travelers with fresh butter, eggs, and milk, and often inviting Jean Rio to visit their homes.

Falling in love with her new country, she harbored no regrets about her decision to leave England. "I often think that there is no person so thoroughly independent as an American farmer," she wrote. "His land is his own; he has beef, mutton, pork, and poultry. He shears his own sheep, his wife spins the wool, dyes it of various colors, and in many cases weaves it into clothes for dresses and other various articles of clothing, blankets, and flannels." All of the homes she had visited were spotless and comfortable, their furniture plain but solid and well crafted.

Passing through a horrible bog in which the wagons sunk to their axles, she dubbed the locale "Devil's Glen." Here she would need to purchase three more yoke of oxen, so depleted was her original stock. For a dollar she also purchased a pig, "which when killed and cleaned weighed 70 pounds," and "three fowls for 25 cents."

Heavy rainfall detained them for two days, and when they were able to continue on it was into the most frightening of landscapes yet encountered. "Now I want you all on my side," she wrote in the diary as if it were a letter meant for friends back in England. "Imagine yourself standing upon a hill as of that in Greenwich Park and looking down into a complete basin, across the bottom of which runs a wide stream of water." Her fear of fording the stream was palpable as she watched the drivers wading up to their waists among the cattle, struggling to keep the wagons afloat: "I confess I trembled as I looked, for I expected no less than to see the wagons run over and crush the cattle during the descent." Safely across, they put their exhausted animals out to graze and waited for the wagons to dry out. The following day brought yet another "quagmire through which the cattle were floundering for nearly four hours," and by the time they reached a dry and flat campsite they had traveled a mere three miles. Here they would spend a full day resting and preparing for what was clearly a more treacherous and daunting expedition than they had expected. It took great effort to move a short distance, and fatigue and frustration began to overtake the party.

They started out again on the morning of May 15 and had traveled less than an hour before they came to "a worse bog than the last if possible." Sixteen oxen were necessary to pull one wagon through—each wagon weighing around two thousand pounds—and so the depleted animals were forced to cross the muddy tract dozens of times. It took four hours for her last wagon to reach the other side. Their camp would be plagued that night with a forceful thunderstorm, and the pelting rain would confine them to their wagons for the entire next day. "In England we know little about thunder," she wrote, "but here among the hills the echoes are so numerous that we frequently hear the second clap begin to rattle before the first has finished."

The next morning an infant in the group died, delaying their travel until midafternoon. By now the plains folded into forests so thick with hickory and oak as to be nearly impassable, the wagons plodding along at a rate of two miles per day. But the weather had improved and the land was now lush with flowers reminiscent of the most cultivated gardens of England. "We are constantly walking over violets, primrose, daisies, bluebells, the lily of the valley, columbines of every shade from the deepest blue to white Virginia stocks in large patches," Jean Rio wrote. "The wild rose, too, is very beautiful, perfuming the air for miles. Onions grow wild by the sides of streams, while in the forests hundreds of trees have their trunks covered by hop or grapevines." Deer, wild turkey, fresh fish, and strawberries now rounded out their daily meals, and the women gathered herbs along the riverbanks to flavor the food.

Increasingly, the days were unbroken by any sign of human habitation, the camp visited by wolves. "We passed . . . a great many of their dens," wrote Jean Rio. "They are simple mounds of earth, which the animals throw up and make their nests in the hollow beneath, leaving an entrance hole on one side." She found the elusive animals more interesting than threatening, even with their incessant nighttime howling, convinced as she was that they lived on small rabbits and squirrels and never attacked "the human race." Thunderstorms and flash floods persisted—"the little gully at the bottom of the hill across which I could have stepped with ease yesterday evening is now a rapid stream at least 20 feet in width." Despite the rattling of the wagons from the thunderclaps, they felt "quite snug in our castles," and when the storms passed the air lit up with fireflies.

By May 22 Jean Rio's party and the other families that had joined them had been on the trail from Alexandria for thirty days, and had advanced only 116 miles. Jean Rio and her fellow travelers were becoming anxious about meeting up with the main company of Saints at Council Bluffs. They couldn't bear the thought of traversing the unknown, dangerous land with only their little band.

The first disaster struck the group when they came to what she called a "slough," or a hollow part of the prairie where the rain settled, "a perfect bog" extending for miles. It became necessary to double- or triple-team the wagons to get them across. As one of Jean Rio's wagons was crossing, the animals revolted and struggled to break free, pulling the wagon toward two women who were holding infants. The oxen stampeded and the wagon ran over one of the women at her waist and the other just above her ankles. Jean Rio's son William rushed to grab the babies, who were uninjured, and then returned to help his mother lift the women out of the bog. "The weight of the wagon was completely forced down on them into the soft mud and providently they had no bones broken," Jean Rio wrote. "Had it been on the hard ground nothing could have saved them from being crushed."

They laid the women side by side on Jean Rio's bed in the wagon and finished crossing. Once safely installed on solid ground they assessed the women's injuries. Mrs. Margett, whose legs had been run over, was sore but otherwise all right. The other victim, Mrs. Bond, was in great pain and unable to move. But even so grave an accident did not detain the group, which was increasingly apprehensive about meeting up with the other Saints. Though the group rarely traveled on Sunday, the leaders now made an exception and decided to push on.

By noon on May 25 they had reached the mouth of the Sheridan River, a daunting body to cross, with a strenuous ascent on the other side. Rainstorms dogged them, slowing their progress, and when an axle on one wagon broke and a wheel of another smashed into the riverbank, they were forced to stop for two days to repair the vehicles. While waiting, the women stocked their wagons with peaches and plums from nearby trees heavy with the fruit and swatted at the latest menace—mosquitoes. Next on their map was the White Breast Creek, which they found to be a "roaring torrent" instead of the small tributary they were expecting. Beginning at four a.m., the men worked in a downpour to build a bridge across the creek, which was rising at the rate of one foot an hour. Four wagons managed to cross before the newly built bridge washed out. It would be hours before a new bridge could be constructed and the remaining wagons conveyed to the other side.

Twelve miles later there was another creek to be forded, and yet another shortly after that. One wagon toppled onto its side but was righted without excessive damage. The group camped, and members picked enough gooseberries "for a pudding" and found mushrooms "four inches long."

On June 3 they traveled one mile before reaching another stream, which took them six hours to cross. Two days later the trail had become virtually impassable, and they camped. Jean Rio walked a half mile to a farmhouse where she hoped to purchase butter. The rains became so heavy she could not return to the camp, "the waters being in the hollows higher than my knees," the thunder and howling wolves so terrifying her that she spent the night with the settlers. "We have had thunderstorms every day for four weeks," she wrote in her diary upon returning to her family.

Three days later they were within view of the tiny settlement of Mount Pisgah, so named by the Mormon prophet and apostle Parley P. Pratt, who, in an Old Testament parallel, likened the spot to the biblical site where Moses envisioned the Promised Land. By this point in the journey, Jean Rio was fatigued and dispirited, her daily entries now successive jottings about creeks and streams all brimming to flood-stage levels; omnipresent thunderstorms; harsh, muddy terrain; waterlogged wagons; and disagreeable traveling companions. "A miserable day altogether," she wrote on June 10. "Got 16 miles, crossed five ravines and four creeks, upset three wagons, got my own bedding wet through, and encamped by ourselves. Surely this is anything but pleasant."

Bickering broke out among the weary Saints. Tempers

flared and the children were now irritable and uncomfortable, their clothing and bedding soggy and cold. Two of the families that had joined Jean Rio's party in Alexandria struck out on their own in six wagons—"much to the satisfaction of us all"—and now the crossing of streams required unloading all belongings from the wagons and carrying them across by hand. "We are reduced to 6 wagons (division having entered among us, the rest have left us at different times)." Four of the wagons belonged to Jean Rio, one carrying her piano, Regent Street finery, and personal items from her London home, the others the furniture and daily necessities for the overland journey. One of the other wagons in the train belonged to the "captain" and one to a family named Jones.

JUNE 14: The storm began about 11 last night and has continued without intermission till nearly noon today. I cannot describe the thunder; it is unlike any I have ever heard. As to the rain upon our wagon covers, I can only compare it to millions of shot falling on sheets of copper. Sleep is out of the question, as well as conversation, for though Aunt [Mary Ann Bateman] and I were in the same wagon it was with difficulty we could make each other heard. Of course there is no chance of proceeding, so I made up my mind to do a day's needlework. Being on top of a hill we are not inconvenienced by the surrounding water. We are 45 miles from human habitation, but we are as merry as larks, and our now small company much happier than when there were so many of us. Our long anxiety is whether we shall be too late to go to the Valley this year.

A stranger from Virginia on horseback joined their camp and told them there were no wagons within seventy miles to the east, so any prospect that others would catch up with them and increase their ranks was diminished. On June 18 Jean Rio saw "a traveler on foot without a coat approaching on the opposite side of the creek." He explained he was walking to St. Louis and had left Council Bluffs two days earlier. There, he told her, two hundred wagons were waiting. "So we shall not be too late at last," wrote Jean Rio.

They pressed on with urgency, but the topography was no more hospitable than before. Crossings now required nine and sometimes twelve yoke of oxen to each wagon, and even then they were obliged "to stop every few minutes for the cattle to recover breath." Once, traveling through darkness, they navigated a "deep serpentine ravine" by the illumination of the lightning. For days they waited for yet another river to recede, and on Sunday held their first prayer meeting in eight weeks. "It seems to have put new life into the men," Jean Rio observed. On June 24 they met a young man traveling from Council Bluffs to Pisgah who imparted the "startling information" that Indians in the near distance were refusing to let Mormons pass through their territory.

Next came a creek seven miles long and too deep to cross, and there was no timber in the area with which to construct a bridge. "Concluded to lay stringers across and draw the wagons over by hand; the oxen could swim over." The teamsters and bullwhackers—hired hands adept at driving teams—surrounded the animals, shouting and whipping, until the recalcitrant beasts finally entered the water. On June 27 the travelers reached the first farm they had seen in more than a hundred miles, and they were given lettuce and spring onions by its owners. Over the next few days they passed more farms, where Jean Rio purchased butter, milk, eggs, and several cows with their calves for thirty dollars, and a "whole sheep for a dollar."

Finally, on July 2, the party reached Council Bluffs, where Jean Rio spent two days meticulously restocking her outfit with enough provisions for the remaining trek to Zion. The party then crossed the "Missouri Bottom," which she described as four miles wide and submerged underwater from the recent heavy rains—"most of the distance the water was running over the axles of the wagons." On July 5 they reached the main camp, where they convened with their shipmates from England who had been met in New Orleans by church leaders who ushered them to Council Bluffs, as well as several more Saints converging from New York, Ohio, and Illinois. The well-known John Brown, who had traversed the plains numerous times, was appointed captain of the entire outfit of forty-two wagons, with four other lieutenants assigned as sub-commanders of ten wagons each, or "tens." The leaders organized the emigrants, mediated disagreements, and determined camp locations. Eager to start, having waited several weeks for them, Captain Brown allowed Jean Rio's party no time to rest before moving out on the final journey. Still, she was so relieved to have joined the large company that a lighthearted optimism overtook her, and the new fear of Indians and other perils as yet unknown temporarily subsided.

CHAPTER SIX

The Crossing

KANESVILLE—ALSO KNOWN AS Winter Quarters, and later called Council Bluffs—had been the command post for Mormon migration west since the spring of 1846. Despite an official treaty between Mormon leader Brigham Young and Missouri officials, hostilities there had escalated, culminating in Young's announcement to his followers in February 1846 that it was time to "flee Babylon by land or by sea." That month, thousands of converts then residing in Missouri, Illinois, and Ohio had begun preparations for the trek to a new Zion in the west. Young had dispatched intermediaries to Washington, D.C., to request government approval for the Saints to settle in Oregon Territory. While in the nation's capital, the Mormon men obtained a copy of John Charles Frémont's report of his recent explorations. That report, one of the first published accounts about the geography, topography, and Indian tribes west of the Missouri River, was a coveted document to the Mormon leader.

Young had heard tales from other explorers about the land around the Great Salt Lake in America's immense Great Basin. "Buffalo, elk, deer, antelope, mountain sheep and goats, white and grizzly bear, beaver, and geese [are] in great abundance" in the area, one of his scouts told him, as well as freshwater streams and a plentiful supply of salt and minerals. Young had procured rare maps of the area and a copy of Lansford W. Hastings's *The Emigrants' Guide to Oregon and California.* He had become attracted to the region near the Great Salt Lake, the site of the vast prehistoric Lake Bonneville. "In the cove of mountains along its eastern shore, the lake is bordered by a plain where the soil is generally good, and a greater part fertile, watered by a delta of prettily timbered streams," Frémont had written. Young had been drawn to its natural isolation, surrounded as it was by snowcapped peaks, salt flats, and high-altitude desert. He saw it as a perfect haven for his persecuted followers.

Even more appealing to Young was the fact that the several thousand square miles of land he intended to claim for his planned nation-state belonged to Mexico, and were therefore outside the dominion of what one of the apostles had called "the bloodthirsty Christians of these United States."

On January 14, 1847, Young had revealed his first, and only recorded, supposed divine revelation, which concerned the thousand-mile pilgrimage to the Great Basin. Called the "Word and Will of the Lord," the prophesy elaborated in specific detail how the emigration should proceed. The emigrants would move not as a whole but as a procession of companies—organized with military precision into hundreds, fifties, and tens—advancing at three-hundred-mile intervals along a chain of far-flung way stations called the "Camp of Israel." Likening his flock to the children of Israel and himself to Moses leading the exodus from Egypt, Young had assured his followers that the angels of God would protect them. Early companies had built roads and bridges along the way for the Saints to follow, and had sown crops to be harvested by later parties.

The first group of 148 Saints, including Brigham Young, had left Winter Quarters in what is now Omaha in the spring of 1847. By July 24 of that year the hardy band had reached their new Jerusalem in the Great Salt Lake Valley. "Zion shall be established in the tops of the mountains and exalted above the hills, and all nations shall flow unto it," one of the first emigrants proclaimed upon arriving in the valley, quoting the Old Testament prophet Isaiah.

Now, exactly four years later, Jean Rio Baker joined with dozens of fellow converts for the final trek to the Promised Land. What had been a relatively lonely and improvised journey thus far now became more methodical and disciplined, an almost military advance. Jean Rio welcomed the extra security as well as the knowledge and experience of the leaders, versed as they were in the location of troublesome Indians, the severity of upcoming obstacles, and other details of the route. Captain Brown had at his disposal rudimentary devices such as sextants and telescopes with which he guided the group by planets identified in the Bible—Orion, Arcturus, and the Pleiades. Primitive barometers and thermometers helped him anticipate weather conditions, and a device that measured the number of revolutions of the front wagon wheel—an inventive Mormon had recently calculated, with amazing accuracy, that 360 revolutions represented one mile—helped him establish his position.

Their first day on the trail took them through country inhabited by Omaha Indians and was marred by a dangerous gorge crossing at the notoriously unsound "Pappea Bridge" nine miles from the Elkhorn River, where several wagons belonging to one of the families were severely damaged. Now reduced to a total of fifty-one wagons—ten were left behind for repairs—they followed what was being called the Mormon Trail, 1,032 rugged miles from Council Bluffs to Salt Lake City, blazed by early trappers and traders. On July 8 they ferried over the Elkhorn, a tributary described by one traveler as "9 rods wide and 3 feet deep." One of the men caught his hand in a chain, breaking a finger and opening a wide gash—an excruciatingly painful injury. With the calmness and efficiency that would come to characterize her, Jean Rio immediately took responsibility for sewing up the wound—the first of many such episodes. Like other women before and after her who made pioneer journeys along the rugged trails of frontier America, she found inner resources and abilities that her previous life had never called upon. Many tasks unthinkable to her as a London matron, tasks daunting to the mostly younger women on the journey, fell to this forty-one-year-old mother of six. If she felt in any way intimidated by the challenges, hesitant to take charge of sometimes life-threatening situations, if the sight of blood and the grimaces or screams of a friend in pain unnerved her, she never even remarked on them in her diary. Like the other women in the wagon train, she found how she could best contribute to the benefit of the common party, and she approached her duties with the poise and command for which she would become known.

Enduring monotony and adversity by turns, and now followed by ravenous mosquitoes, which left angry, itching welts, the party made its way to the Platte River, where they saw their first Indian grave. They camped on the riverbank in what is now eastern Nebraska (named for the Oto Indian word *nebrathka,* meaning "flat water"). They would traverse this most desultory of rivers dozens of times over hundreds of miles in the weeks to come. "A nothing river," the novelist James Michener describes it. "Too thick to drink, too thin to plow."

The party halted for an entire day so that the men could repair damage to the axles of several wagons while the women "took the opportunity to wash up our dirty linen." When they proceeded the weather had turned unbearably hot, the trail a sandy loam that swallowed the wheels. Passing another Indian grave, the emigrants became increasingly nervous, mindful of rumors they had heard about a great convocation among Indian tribes determined to settle territorial issues among themselves and with a U.S. government that had exacerbated tension and violence on all sides. The chiefs and warriors of the Pawnee, Shoshone, Cheyenne, Sioux, Crow, Arapaho, Comanche, and Kiowa nations were converging that summer from all directions to meet at Fort Laramie, most of them camping nearby at various locations along the Platte.

On the evening of July 12, the emigrants stopped beside a small lake. Jean Rio ventured into the countryside to gather a "red root" that tasted like spinach and that she boiled for her family. She had taken to venturing alone into the countryside, so compelled was she by the landscape; her outings became so routine that Captain Brown always made sure she was back among them before moving the wagons out. After dinner a group of wagons approached the camp from the west, the travelers asking if they could accompany the Mormon entourage. "We now number 54," she wrote that night, "three others have joined us since we left the Missouri River. These newcomers had started for Oregon, but had been attacked by Indians who had stolen some of their oxen and driven away the rest."

The next day the party came upon ten of the "strangers' missing cattle, which was quite a God-send to them." One of the men shot a ten-pound fish in a nearby stream; it fed Jean Rio's entire family. "We are now on the Plains in the Pawnee country," she noted on July 14. They reached the site where the Indians had attacked their new companions, and found abandoned yokes and bows that would serve as welcome replacement parts for her damaged carriages.

Crossing deep chasms and swamps, climbing steep riverbanks to camp on high ground, the party was plagued yet again by violent thunderstorms. Jean Rio rose on the morning of July 18 to the sound of a raging river that required the men to build a bridge. Several wagons were damaged in the crossing; the party was forced to halt for two days to fix them. One of the women who had traveled with Jean Rio from London died suddenly, though she had seemed to be in perfect health only days before. Jean Rio and her sister-in-law, Mary Ann, "laid her out and sewed her body up in a sheet." The party climbed to the summit of a nearby hill to bury the woman at sunset, and there found the graves of five other people who had died in the same locale.

For days the party continued across the wearisome prairie, lumbering along like a tiny moving village, the tedium broken only by "frogs, hares, and doves." Jean Rio came upon an elk skull with an ominous message written in pencil, a warning to be on the lookout for Indians who were preying on emigrant parties. The wagon train proceeded slowly against a blasting headwind, all of the livestock suffering now from the heat and exertion. On July 24, "the hottest day we have had," one of her oxen dropped dead. Halfway across what would become Nebraska Territory they came to Fort Kearny, named for the general who had commanded the American army in the Mexican War, which had ended three years earlier. There, for thirty dollars, Jean Rio was able to purchase a new ox.

As they crept their way west they came upon their first herd of the legendary buffalo that were said to turn the prairie black. The animals were every bit as magnificent as lore had suggested, but they added yet another bit of trepidation to a company whose nerves were frayed. Stampedes, random and chaotic in their disastrous consequences, were among the most feared of all hazards on the trail, and the presence of buffalo was but one more threat to a jittery team of oxen, horses, and mules that routinely spooked at unknown elements. "Our Encampment . . . was called to pass through one of those Horrid scenes to day which are so much dredded by all Emigrating

Companies," Mormon apostle Wilford Woodruff had written the previous summer.

> No person who has not Experienced or witnessed one of those dredful scenes cannot form any Correct idea of them . . . for to behold 30 or 40 ox teams [with] from 2 to five yoke of oxen in each team attached to a family waggon of goods & women & Children All in an instant . . . each running their own way, roaring, bellowing rolling & tumbling over each other waggons upsetting smashing their wheels Exles & tongues spilling the goods women & Child in the street, for the next teams to trample under their feet as they roar & charge on their way with their yokes bows & chains flying in evry direction. Little can be done at such times ownly for each one to dodge the best He can & save his own life if possible.

Captain Brown, who had crossed the plains five times, told Jean Rio that he had seen herds numbering more than ten thousand. One of her sons shot a young buffalo, and the party enjoyed their first fresh meat in weeks. But the meal could not compensate for the trouble caused by the herd. "Stragglers are apt to run in among our cattle," she wrote, "terrifying them very much, and it has been all the horsemen could do to prevent their doing mischief."

On July 30 they approached another company, which was made up of 115 wagons. Jean Rio recognized two of her former shipmates, and she swapped tales of the trail with them. The other party had had a much more trying journey, their cattle stampeded by Indians and a woman among them run over and killed. The two companies advanced on the trail within a mile of each other, hoping to find strength and protection in numbers. The men and boys in Jean Rio's party killed a buffalo one evening, but darkness fell before they were able to cut up the animal. They returned at first light to find the entire carcass picked clean by wolves, only a few bones remaining. But that morning they shot two more, and Jean Rio would carry the hides with her to Utah, where she would turn them into sumptuous blankets. The abundant buffalo dung (or "bois de vache," as they called the chips), objectionable at first, was soon seen as welcome fuel, burning clean and quickly and eliminating the sometimes impossible task of finding firewood.

The flat land gave way to sand hills crawling with "thousands of lizards, snakes, and grasshoppers," the oxen tripping in the dirt, kicking up dust into the faces of the emigrants. Jean Rio found the landscape "wild and romantic," and often wandered off by herself to bask in the inspiring sight. The wagons forged up the Platte River valley through the gently rolling hills of sand, making their way to the upper Missouri Basin. She saw two more graves and, noting the names of the deceased in her journal, she wondered how those pioneers had died. The possibilities seemed endless. She knew that most injuries were caused by wagon accidents, often involving women and girls whose unsuitable dresses, cumbersome hoops, and long petticoats became caught in the wheel spokes, pulling them to gruesome deaths. The American feminist

Amelia Bloomer had been advocating full trousers—known as bloomers—worn under shorter skirts. But such reformed fashion—called the "Move toward Rational Dress"—was far from acceptable in the patriarchal Mormon society.

Still more travelers were kicked or gored by oxen, poisoned by rattlesnakes or spiders, or stricken by the most dreaded disease of all: cholera. Women died in childbirth and newborns failed to thrive. Children were jostled off the wagons' box seats to be run over by the wagons. Drowning in raging torrents often occurred, and dehydration afflicted the less sturdy. The most dangerous animal of the American continent, the grizzly bear, also was responsible for human casualties.

The threat of massacre at the hands of Indians was much exaggerated. Indians throughout the nation had killed only thirty-seven emigrants during a one-year period in 1849 that saw an estimated 14,500 people traverse the continent to the West Coast, of whom several hundred died of accidents and natural causes along the way. But that was enough for the myth of the "savage" to prevail, causing notable anxiety.

The trail was now comparatively easy, and to the children the journey seemed an endless picnic of fun and adventure. Sleeping outdoors was exciting; the howling coyotes had become welcome as fellow inhabitants of the lonely prairie. The children found plenty of playmates and invented games along the way. They chased groundhogs and lizards, hiked bluffs and splashed in streams, cut their names into rocks, and played hide-and-seek. To them, the landscape was a boundless natural zoo. Some of the families had brought their family pets—cats and dogs—which could often be seen peering out of the backs of wagons. A member of the company gave ten-year-old Elizabeth a puppy, which delighted and amused her and her younger brothers, John Edye and Charles West. For all the hardship, Jean Rio loved seeing her children so happy, so alive and vivacious in these foreign but natural surroundings.

Evening thundershowers left the road heavy in early morning, but the arid days dried it out quickly. Dramatic bluffs and rock formations rose out of the ground on both sides of the river, the topography now unlike anything the emigrants had ever seen. For Jean Rio, as for others, encountering the majesty of the landscape was a profound emotional experience. She poured out her awe and love in lush, lavish descriptions of fiery sunsets and swollen streams, miragelike vistas and violent weather. The travelers relished the days when they had moderate conditions, certain as they were that they would soon face the most arduous and challenging part of the journey as the gentle buttes melded first into foothills and then into the ten-thousand-foot mountain passes they could begin to see in the distance. A band of Sioux Indians joined them, "very fine looking fellows, and very gaily attired. The dresses of the women . . . nearly covered with beadwork." The trail followed the river north toward Fort Laramie, which had been built in 1841 by the American Fur Company; there Jean Rio paid sixty-five dollars for a new yoke of oxen and "four fine hams."

At night the cattle strayed, and precious hours were lost rounding them up at dawn. Good grass for grazing the livestock was getting more and more difficult to find. The party bridged the North Platte River near what is now Casper,

Wyoming, in search of pasture and found themselves surrounded by ridges covered with cedar and pine. "A very hard road all day; crossed some mountains. The view from the top no pen can describe. We managed to get 20 miles, but it was hard work; did not get to camp till 11 o'clock," Jean Rio noted. Along the way she saw four dead oxen, along with remnants of wagons, wheels, and axles, "the results of former accidents." But the signs of destruction were mitigated by "loads of cherries and currants" on the hillsides. They stopped on the afternoon of August 19 to repair wagons and allow Jean Rio to employ her developing medical skills by acting as a midwife. "Sister gave birth to a daughter," she wrote that evening, and proudly recorded that the newborn was "doing well." (Among the Mormon brethren, the women were referred to as "Sisters" and the men as "Brothers.")

The dust along the route filled their lungs, and what she described as "horrible roads" compelled them to cross the North Platte twice in one day. "Very hard and bad traveling; deep ravines," she wrote on August 23, finding great solace the next day, a Sunday, on which an elder of the church "preached of the first principles of the Gospel of Christ." Again she was called to deliver a baby. She now accepted her role as midwife, having become expert at inducing a baby down the birth canal, comforting a distraught young woman, snipping the umbilical cord, extracting the placenta by coaxing contractions from a depleted mother, and stimulating the newborn to breathe on its own. "I was sent for to go to Sister Henderson, who had been sick for two days. In one hour I was able to assist her in giving birth to a daughter, but the mother is so much exhausted that I fear she will not rally again." Now, with no expertise or training to guide her, she felt unexpectedly responsible for two women and two infants, all four struggling for life, for a chance of survival on this harsh American frontier.

On August 26 the wagons were halted to give the two young mothers a chance to recover their strength and nurse their babies. As Jean Rio attended to them, Captain Brown sent a hunting party out to find fresh meat for the company, sustenance that it was hoped would fortify the new mothers as well as improve the morale of the rest.

"Sister Henderson died today at noon," she wrote. "We buried her at 9 p.m. She left seven children."

This was the first mother Jean Rio had lost, and she was devastated. Still, she took refuge in stoic understatement, seeking the place where her efforts ended and her faith began. She wondered if she could have changed the outcome, and in the end found the only solace possible—in the belief in a divine plan.

Mourning for Sister Henderson was cut short when Captain Brown announced on the morning of August 28 that Indians surrounded them. The wagons had to be brought close together, and they would move forward as a slow, unified body. Jean Rio could see an army of nearly one hundred warriors a mile in the distance. "Our men at once loaded their guns so as to be in readiness in case of an attack," she wrote. Girding for battle, the party approached the band warily. But as the emigrants came nearer, the Indians' formation opened to let them pass without incident. "They made a grand appearance, all on horseback . . . some with lances, others with guns or bows and arrows." Colored ponies carried the Indians' tents. "The men passed on one side of us, the women and children on the other." Among the Indians, sitting in a buggy with a toddler between his knees, was the U.S. government Indian agent. He told Jean Rio that this was a detachment from the more than three thousand Shoshone encamped on the bank of the Sweetwater River twenty miles to the southwest. They were en route to "the great council of various tribes to endeavor to settle their differences and bury the tomahawk," he told her.

From there the trail entered the Rocky Mountains and Jean Rio got her first sight of snowcapped Laramie Peak in the distance, a daunting portent of the days to come. She "walked under overhanging rocks, which seemed only to need the pressure of a finger to send them down headlong." Likening them to old English castles, she gathered relics of silver and iron ore. "Our road is so steep as to seem almost like going down a staircase," she wrote. She was intrigued by "the property of the atmosphere" that revealed far-off landmarks in sharp focus. "While crossing the plains, I have frequently noticed different objects, which I imagined I should have little trouble in reaching on foot, and on inquiring the distance, have been told they were perhaps 20 or 30 miles distant. In particular, one morning while at breakfast I observed a rather singularly shaped hill directly in our road, and as usual felt an instant desire to mount the summit." Thinking it two or three miles away, she decided to leave camp ahead of the company in order to "view the surrounding country from the top." But Captain Brown stopped her. "If we are able to reach that hill tomorrow night," he said, "I shall be very satisfied with our teams, as it is at least 26 miles before us."

The oxen had been pushed beyond fatigue, their hooves so tender the animals refused to move, and it became necessary to halt for several days as they regained their strength. "Remained in camp all day to give the sick oxen a rest," she wrote on September 5. "Killed three antelopes and caught a lot of fish." When they resumed their journey they could travel only a few hours a day, crossing a sixty-mile stretch of rocky ridges called Hell's Reach. "The campsites were bad, the water worse, and stretches of alkali flats soon slowed the poor oxen down," according to one account of the infamous section of trail. "Many were driven beyond their normal strengths and 'gave up the ghost' at this point. The stench of dead animals was ever present."

Then came Devil's Backbone, where one of Jean Rio's oxen died, apparently from ingesting some Indian war paint. Because of the scarcity of grass for the animals, it became necessary to push on twenty miles without stopping. They proceeded south along the Sweetwater River—named Eau Sucrée by early French trappers grateful for its sweet and clear taste after the murky Platte. Flowing ninety-three miles to South Pass, three feet deep and seventy feet wide, the most welcome of all rivers would be crossed by Jean Rio three times in one day. She traversed the Continental Divide at the 7,500-foot-high South Pass.

On September 8 the party encountered John M. Bernhisel,

a Mormon diplomat who was heading to Washington, D.C., from Salt Lake City. Two years earlier Congress had refused to acknowledge the "State of Deseret," the independent theocracy created by Brigham Young on that huge chunk of territory. Instead, Congress had established Utah Territory, and President Millard Fillmore had appointed Young as governor. The new territory was smaller than Deseret but still an expansive landmass comprising what is now Utah, Nevada, and a portion of western Colorado. Though Young and his followers had deeply resented the federal government's interference in their affairs, the prophet would use his new title and standing to his own advantage. Bernhisel had been elected the first congressman from the territory, which covered more than 200,000 square miles. "All the news he brought us was of a cheering kind," Jean Rio wrote of making Bernhisel's acquaintance.

That week, a milk cow kicked a member of the party, a young girl, breaking her leg. Jean Rio helped the girl's father examine the protruding bone, force it back into position, and fashion a splint with timber. Two men on mules overtook the group and reported that more than a thousand Indian lodges had been situated near Fort Laramie, and all on the trail were apprehensive that trouble was brewing. "Two Shoshones had been killed by a party of Cheyennes," Jean Rio noted. "The Shoshones in return had slaughtered twenty-seven out of thirty Cheyennes they had fallen in with on their way to the Great Council of the Tribes. Poor prospect, this of Peace among them, as these thirty were actually delegates from their own people." Fortunately, she and her party had pushed west beyond the conflict.

On the morning of September 13, a "general strike" broke out among the teamsters traveling with a member of the party. "There has been dissatisfaction for some weeks, owing to the scantiness and inferior quality of their rations," Jean Rio wrote. The teamsters' employer refused to amend the situation. The men "shouldered their blankets and set off" on foot. Captain Brown overtook the "mutineers" and told them that if they returned he would oversee an investigation of the matter. He then provided them with a tent and plenty of buffalo robes, and they agreed to rejoin the outfit.

Jean Rio's sons went hunting for game, as the family's provisions were dwindling, but came back empty-handed. Three supply wagons from Salt Lake City approached them, and the group cheered for what they anticipated would be much-needed food sent to them from Utah. Unfortunately, the supply train had already sold everything to emigrants ahead of them, but the leader promised that wagons laden with flour were en route to meet them. Disappointed and hungry, the party continued along the Big Sandy River to its conjunction with the Green River, passing through spectacularly beautiful country. "We were just the ones to appreciate it," Jean Rio wrote, "having seen nothing but sand and wild sage for three hundred miles."

They forded the cottonwood-lined Green River—"a wide rushing stream, clear as crystal"—where Jean Rio observed a white substance shimmering among the pebbles on the riverbank. "I managed to scramble down to the water's edge, and on taking up some, first looking at it and then tasting it, found it to be pure salt." As they sat down to dinner the evening of

September 15, a man from a trading post two miles away joined them. He had come to inquire if they wanted any cattle or other provisions. "What have you got?" Jean Rio asked him. "Bacon and whiskey, Madam," he answered. "Any butter?" "No butter," he responded. "Any groceries or fresh meat?" "No, Madam, but there is plenty at Fort Bridger fifty miles further."

Still, she sent her oldest son, Walter, with him to the trading post, so eager had they become for any fresh food. Walter returned with some bacon. He described the man's "trading post" as a group of huts inhabited by Snake Indians who had among them four Ute women who had been captured and made prisoners while children. The white trader had lived with the Indians for the past fifteen years and was one of four white men who resided there with their Indian wives. "Each had his own habitation, several hundred head of cattle, and 150 horses, and seemed to be very happy in their wilderness way of life."

On September 19 the party reached Fort Bridger, where Jean Rio happily purchased forty pounds of fresh beef at ten cents a pound. "I never saw finer in the London markets, and that is saying a great favor," she noted. They continued on, ascending the rim of the Great Basin two days later. A gentle but incessant rain kept the dust down, and she described the scenery as "sublime . . . our road being between and around high mountains." Climbing one mountain required ten yoke to each wagon, but the end felt near, so morale was high.

Her pregnant daughter-in-law, Eliza, was suddenly very ill, and Jean Rio worried about a premature birth. Just as she feared, Eliza went into labor in the middle of the night. At daybreak on September 22 Jean Rio delivered her first grandchild, a tiny boy who would be named Henry William Rio Baker. The Baker children were overjoyed by this new addition, so close to Zion.

"I have some fear for its life," Jean Rio wrote, "but I do hope our Heavenly Father will spare it to us and make it a blessing to us all and an honorable member of His Kingdom." Remembering the burial at sea of her small son, Josiah, she felt the imminence of death all around her. While she noted the occurrences in terms that today would sound archaic and even naïve, her endless appeals to God at such times, and her absolute faith in a divine plan, were common and universal to Christians of her time and place. She had committed herself and her family to the hands of a higher power. She had been converted not to Christianity but to a deeper notion of the "everlasting," and she sought solace in that conception when the world seemed most precarious.

The travelers rested for three days so Eliza could recover from the delivery and nurture her newborn. Jean Rio lost another ox to poison but was so enraptured with the birth of the baby and the proximity of Salt Lake City that she considered it but a minor inconvenience. She wrote that the country had been "beyond description for wilderness and beauty. We are indeed among the everlasting hills." Still, there were challenges ahead. Weaving its way through a ninety-mile chain of cliffs that cut into the Wasatch Range of the Rockies, the party reached the summit of the Bear Divide, at 7,245 feet, on September 27. There Jean Rio got her first glimpse of the Great Salt Lake Valley. Greeting the group at the top were several Mormon men with fresh teams to assist in the sheer and precarious descent.

Jean Rio took her new grandson into her arms and carried him four miles rather than risk having him ride in a wagon that might overturn. She would remember the joy of that moment for the rest of her life, triumphantly carrying the newborn Henry William Rio Baker all the way to the magnificent valley of the Great Salt Lake. Eliza and another woman who had just given birth—"the two ladies 'in the straw'"— were the only members of the party to remain in the wagons. As Jean Rio reached the bottom, she panicked when she looked up to see the wagons rushing down even though the wheels had been locked. Miraculously they all arrived intact. "We are now at the entrance of a narrow defile between rocks measuring 800 feet perpendicular height, with a serpentine stream running through it which we shall have to cross nineteen times."

An hour after starting out the following day, they came to an abysmal ravine "over which was thrown an apology for a bridge." It was the most rugged terrain since leaving Council Bluffs, and Eliza "suffered much from the roughness of the road." Captain Brown informed them that the next day would be even worse, as indeed it was.

"Of all the splendid scenery and awful roads that have ever been seen since Creation, I think this day's journey has beaten them all," Jean Rio noted on September 28. They had camped the night before at the foot of a mountain, which they then ascended. "This was hard enough on our poor worn-out animals, but the road after was completely covered with stones as large as bushel boxes, stumps of trees with here and there mud holes in which our poor oxen sunk to the knees. Added to this was the Canyon Creek—a stream of water running at the bottom of the ravine, interlacing our road in such a zigzag fashion that we had to ford it sixteen times at a descent of 15 to 20 feet, and of course an equal ascent that in some places was nearly perpendicular." By now she had lost more than a dozen oxen during the trek.

Enveloped by mountains of solid rock, she marveled at the huge evergreen trees growing in the crevices, and the building-size boulders that had tumbled down in landslides, sometimes completely blocking the trail. "In one spot the rocks had the appearance of a ruinous gateway through which we had to pass," she wrote. "The opening was very narrow, only one wagon could go along at a time, and that along the bed of the Canyon Creek, which seems to have forced its way through the opening I have described."

The trail then turned and passed under massive overhanging rocks. "The grandeur of the scenery to my mind takes away all fear, and while standing in admiration of the view Milton's expressions in *Paradise Lost* came forcibly to my recollection: 'These are thy glorious works, Parent of good in wisdom hath thou made them all.' " In that moment she forgot all the hardship of her pilgrimage. "Suddenly, I heard a sound as of rushing water on my left hand, and looking in that direction I observed that the mountain stream buried itself among some bushes, and sure enough there was the prettiest waterfall I had seen yet. The cataract in itself was comprised of fifteen separate falls over as many pieces of rock." Struck with "both

On entering the long-sought valley of Zion, Mormon "Saints" like Jean Rio were greeted with the majestic sight of the Great Salt Lake. Always impressed by the physical grandeur of the American West, she was in awe of the setting of her new home.

awe and delight," she stayed behind until the teamsters yelled at her that she was dangerously delinquent.

They came upon a row of seven wagons, each with a broken wheel or axle. Continuing on, they reached yet another party of ten wagons in similar disrepair. "We picked our way as well we could, and at about sunset we emerged from the canyon and caught a faint view of our destined home." The party camped in a hollow at the entrance to the Great Salt Lake Valley. Exhausted, Jean Rio joined Eliza in a wagon. The young woman was in extreme distress from the jolting of the day's travel. Jean Rio encouraged her with the knowledge that the following day would be the last of their journey. "Thank God . . . it is over now," she wrote in her diary that final evening. "They tell us that five miles tomorrow will bring us to the said Salt Lake City, and after crossing a hill, at whose base we are now resting, we shall have a road as smooth as a bowling green."

She rose the morning of September 29 "with a thankful heart that our travels were nearly finished." After breakfast she attended to her "two patients," Eliza and the baby, who were both getting along better than could have been expected. Impatient to see her new home, Jean Rio clambered to the top of the hill the wagons would soon climb. There before her she saw the city "which was laid out in squares, or blocks as they call them here, each containing ten acres and divided into eight lots, each lot having one house." She stood speechless and stared. "I can hardly analyze my feelings, but I think my prevailing ones were joy and gratitude for the protecting care God had over me and mine during our long and perilous journey."

CHAPTER SEVEN

A Life of Toil

JEAN RIO'S ENTOURAGE was an eye-catching sight in primitive, poverty-ridden Salt Lake City. The special wagon carrying the piano, the inventory of household fur nishings and clothing, and the obvious refinement of the Baker family members caught the attention of many in the set- tlement now inhabited by some five thousand souls. This was a woman of unmistakable means, a woman whose back- ground and cultivation set her apart from most of the Saints who had migrated since 1847.

Jean Rio carried with her a letter of introduction to a Mrs. Wallace, whose husband she had met in London, where he was serving as a missionary. Mrs. Wallace received the family hos- pitably, offering to enclose their wagons and livestock within her property. Several curious neighbors came to welcome them, and Jean Rio set out to find a home for herself and her family as quickly as possible. "We have been living in our wag- ons 24 weeks this day," she wrote, "and I shall be glad to get in a habitation where I can sit down and think over all that has passed on this lengthened journey."

The very day Brigham Young's party had descended into

the Salt Lake Valley in July 1847, they had unhitched their wagons and plowed the soil. Sowing potatoes, corn, beans, and peas, they had set out to tame the desert, irrigating the prehistoric lake bed by digging ditches to direct the summer mountain runoff into the new fields. Lake Bonneville had once covered twenty thousand square miles with fresh water, but it was now reduced to a vast expanse of salt flats.

Young had addressed his small contingent the following day, setting out the laws of his empire in this land of Canaan. The covenants—some tacit then, articulated later—would include the most controversial of church doctrines: "celestial marriage," or polygamy, and "blood atonement," a ritualized form of murder in which the killer provides his victim with eternal salvation by slitting his throat. There would be no tolerance of those weak in the faith, he had warned his followers. From that day forward Young would preside over an autocratic theocracy, a socialist utopia increasingly militaristic and secessionist in the years to come. From here he would usher in the "Dispensation of the Fullness of Times" that was to signal Christ's return, gathering the remnants of Israel to the "only true church" as prophesied by Joseph Smith.

Guided by the hand of God, he said, he used a sacred "divining rod" to select a forty-acre lot as the site for a massive temple and designed the city at the foot of the Wasatch Mountains. Beginning at the temple, 132-foot-wide streets were laid out following the cardinal points of the compass. Young divided the two-square-mile city into lots of one and a quarter acres, eight lots in a block for homes with individual yards, designed so that no house directly faced another. A nearby six-square-mile enclosure—the "Big Field"—was platted into parcels ranging from five to eighty acres for farming. As noted earlier, there would be no private ownership of property in what one of Young's clerks described as this "place where the land is acknowledged to belong to the Lord," and each man would be assigned two plots, one for a home and one for a farm. But the plan for a rich widow such as Jean Rio was less clear, so rare were her circumstances in the new Zion. There was no place in this society for unmarried women.

The agrarian method projected by Young was based upon the industriousness and perfection of the bee. The beehive was the symbol of the Saints. "The communal food gatherers, or farmer bees," writes David Bigler in his book *Forgotten Kingdom*, "were to live in the city, or hive, and harvest food from assigned plots in nearby fields for central storage from which all would share, according to their needs." Under the "Law of Consecration," Saints were soon expected to give over all of their property to the church, for the building of the Kingdom, which would then oversee their livelihood. The men could keep parcels of land conveyed to them as long as they remained faithful, tithing members of the church. The strict method of tithing included 10 percent of all income and 10 percent of all produce raised, which went into the personal coffers of Brigham Young as trustee for the church, and were used in part for the support of his mansion and plural wives. "He renders no account of the funds that come into his hands," wrote a nineteenth-century Mormon journalist, "but tells the faithful that they are at perfect liberty to examine the books at any moment."

A Harper's Weekly *illustration of Salt Lake City circa 1858 showing the meticulously designed city much as Jean Rio first saw it when she arrived in the Mormon capital in 1851.*

There is no indication from Jean Rio's writings that she anticipated such a scenario. How much money she brought with her is unknown, but of course in London she had inherited a small fortune. "Different methods were used on different people to relieve them of their wealth," says Bigler.

Whatever the state of her finances, Jean Rio had arrived in Utah Territory during what Mormon historians would later call the "Stone of Daniel" period. The Saints believed they were fulfilling the prophecy of the biblical Daniel as he intrepreted Nebuchadnezzar's dream: "And in the days of these kings shall the God of heaven set up a Kingdom, which shall never be destroyed; and the kingdom shall not be left to other people; it shall break in pieces and consume all these kingdoms, and it shall stand for ever." This theocratic state was clearly on a collision course with the government of the United States.

"I have purchased a small house with an acre of garden attached to it," Jean Rio wrote on October 6. "There are only four rooms, but we can manage for the winter." How different this home was from her London town house, and from the opulent residence of her childhood. What a stark contrast was this arid landscape from the rainy, verdant city of her girlhood. But she had long since reconciled herself to a new life of simplicity and struggle and had not yet encountered the series of disappointments and betrayals that would later make her yearn for an idealized England. "The garden is in good cultivation," she went on, "and has growing a patch of Indian corn, also potatoes, cabbage, carrots, parsnips, beets, and tomatoes watered by a little stream. The house is 40 feet from the road and fronts the public square." She also bought a "heifer, which supplies us with milk." All members of her party were in good health except for Eliza, who remained weak. Even the "small and delicate" newborn was beginning to flourish.

Having acquired a taste for wild scenery and having a natural penchant for adventure, she was settled in Salt Lake City less than a week when she ventured out into the wilderness. "I had a wish to visit a sulphur lake four miles distant," she wrote. She asked her two oldest sons to yoke some oxen to one of her wagons for the day trip. Winding along a stream that followed the Wasatch foothills, she could smell the mineral water miles before they reached it. "We managed with some difficulty to get close to the opening and there, sure enough, was the water boiling furiously and of a bright green color." From that vantage point she could see the Great Salt Lake in the distance, its surface covered with "tens of thousands" of wild ducks. But the outing would prove singular, as her days in Utah Territory would soon be ruled by drudgery, leaving little opportunity for the recreational explorations and wilderness treks she had brightly anticipated.

Now she was faced with building a future. While she knew nothing about farming, other life skills had been honed on the overland journey. Like most pioneer women she had learned how to address myriad exigencies as well as everyday concerns. She could poultice wounds, sew up lacerations, treat dysentery and colic, and lay out a corpse. She learned how to create teas and salves from the native herbs and roots. She had by default become an experienced midwife, having delivered babies during the overland trek. She came to see these new-found abilities as a calling; her confidence and her competence in delicate and demanding tasks that she had never performed before gave her a sense that she was doing this by divine guidance and inspiration. Her sons would learn to farm and hunt the deer, elk, and antelope that roamed the nearby mountains, while she mastered the domestic skills needed for the self-sufficiency of her family. Having witnessed the killing, skinning, and butchering of game animals on the trail, she and her sons would put their knowledge to use with the cattle, chickens, hogs, and sheep they raised. She would learn how to preserve, can, dry, and store the fruits and vegetables they harvested, and how to turn fresh milk into butter and cheese. The mundane chore of laundering took on massive dimensions as she tried to furnish clean clothing and linen for her family—a never-ending battle in the dusty environs of the high desert. Drawing countless buckets of water from a stream, heating them over open fires, scrubbing the increasingly threadbare clothing with the soap she had made, and then employing what a granddaughter would call those "instruments of torture designed by men for women to use," she would iron them stiff. She learned to sew, turning buffalo skins into luxuriant robes and blankets, deer and cow hides into rugs for her dwelling.

Aside from Brigham Young's elaborate mansion, the Lion House—so named because the corpulent, stentorian Young was called "the Lion of the Lord"—and the residences of his affluent apostles, Jean Rio's home, with its English furniture, Persian rugs, bone china, and sterling flatware, was among the best appointed in the city. The elaborately carved and exquisitely inlaid Collard & Collard piano was the centerpiece of her parlor. What little leisure time she had revolved around music, reading, and writing. She sang in the church choir, played the piano for her family and new friends, read from her leatherbound volumes of Shakespeare and other classics, wrote letters back to England, and continued her diary. She also took on the responsibility of educating her young children, who stood out among their peers for their manners and impeccable dress.

She noted the great disparity between the city's inhabitants. A few, like her, lived in relatively large and comfortable adobe and brick structures. Most of the others occupied crude hovels, many of which were dugouts carved into the hillside, their roofs covered with willow branches, dirt, and canvas. There were no windows or doors, and a hanging cloth was meant to keep out the cold. Infested by rattlesnakes and insects, the willow shanties often provided shelter for large families in a two-hundred-square-foot space. One pioneer called her home the "Castle of Spiders."

Particularly disturbing to Jean Rio was the status of women, who were unable to vote, to hold office, or even to express opinions without facing public opprobrium. For a woman of her breeding, education, and professional experience, it was a rude awakening. Most of the women in Salt Lake City lived in squalor reminiscent of the worst of London. "This is a hideous place," wrote one of her contemporaries. "Some days ago, I killed a rattlesnake with my rolling pin, as he came crawling down the steps. I was just cooking supper and the baby was on the floor or rather the ground, for we have no other floor. I was badly frightened. A few days ago, while keeping the flies off the baby's face as he slept on an improvised bed on the floor, I discovered, to my horror, a large tarantula crawling toward the child."

Some settlers managed to build primitive log cabins, which brought their own form of misery. The timber was a haven for bugs, which attracted hundreds of mice. "Sometimes as many as 60 would be caught before going to bed," wrote one settler. The rain from summer thundershowers and melting winter snows routinely trickled through the willow roofs, turning the cabins' dirt floors into a muddy mess.

It soon became alarmingly apparent to Jean Rio that the rumors of polygamy, long denied by the church, were indeed true. "Celestial marriage" and "eternal progression" were fundamental tenets of early church doctrine, and high officials had been covertly practicing them since the mid-1830s, though "the Principle," as it was euphemistically called, was not formally sanctioned. Long after Joseph Smith had taken polygamously several of what would eventually number forty-eight wives, the church publicly disavowed the doctrine's existence. The revelation of the "Law of Jacob"—named for the Old Testament polygamist—had not been presented officially as a commandment from God until 1842, and even then was practiced in secrecy. Afraid he would incur the wrath of the "Gentiles," Smith had privately revealed the "blessing" to his intimates one by one. Among the chosen few was the apostle Brigham Young, who, upon learning of the revelation, polygamously took a second wife within weeks.

In August 1843 the controversial revelation had been committed to writing and presented to the church's high council. Most men were shocked and conflicted—to say nothing of the wives, who were now expected to share their husbands. But untold numbers acquiesced with a growing commitment to God's divine plan. "Spiritual wifery," as it was called, was a crucial and urgent component of the faith's concept of "eternal progression." This core doctrine, upon which the family values, patriarchal traditions, and early rituals of the religion were based, had at its root the journey to the "Celestial Kingdom"—"the pinnacle of post-mortal existence," as one scholar describes it, where the "faithful will evolve into gods in their own right and come to rule universes of their own." According to the doctrine, Joseph Smith, Brigham Young, and all the other Mormon male luminaries would progress until they were equal in power and stature with God. That all male believers were on the road to godhood, that a heaven existed where all men could be saved and then go on to create their own worlds, was a compelling notion to the faithful. To Jean Rio it was an abomination, and its concealment was one of many lies she now realized she had been told by the missionaries.

In the patriarchy of Mormondom, a woman could enter this eternal realm only as an appendage to a man, so it became a man's ecclesiastical duty to take as many women "through the veil" as possible. A woman found no eternal salvation without being "sealed" to a "worthy male," who was by definition a priest. "Hence all true Mormons are Priests, and women really do not amount to much in themselves, as they have no souls of their own," recalled Mary Ettie V. Smith in the narrative *Fifteen Years Among the Mormons*. An unattached woman faced the unappealing prospect of being lodged for eternity in the limbo of the "Telestial Kingdom," what one writer has called "the lowest rung of the Mormon hereafter . . . a paradise for Gentiles."

Evoking a biblical justification for "the Principle," Young avowed that God himself was a mortal being residing on a planet orbiting a star called Kolob, where he was sexually active with his first wife, the Heavenly Mother, and his other wives; that Adam was a polygamist, and Eve but one of his many wives; and that Jesus had slept with Mary Magdelene and had multiple wives as well. "They [the Mormons] are Jews in their theocracy," wrote the celebrated but controversial nineteenth-century British author Sir Richard Francis Burton in *The City of the Saints,* expressing the dismay of many English and European intellectuals at a Mormonism that seemed to them a caricature of Old Testament religions. "They are Christians inasmuch as they base their faith upon the Bible, and hold to the divinity of Christ, the fall of man, the atonement and regeneration. They are Moslems in their views of the inferior status of womankind, in their polygamy, and in their resurrection of the material body."

According to Mormon doctrine there were to be three types of marriage: the first, secular marriage being for "time," the second for "time and eternity," and the third for "eternity." Thus the doctrine proclaimed that for a man to reach the pinnacle of eternal bliss he must marry three times, each wife representing a jewel in his kingly crown. Some faithful Saints eagerly adopted this matrimonial system as the requisite avenue to godhood in the hereafter. Meanwhile, to serve their temporal interests here on earth, they were careful and calculating in their selection of wives, seeking mates who would advance their business or household interests. "Each wife would be chosen to serve in a different capacity," according to one account of the arrangement. "There were cooks, laundresses, hostesses, and mothers, all profitable to the husband. It was less expensive to marry a woman than to hire her for wages." Viewed as the property of their husbands, often referred to as "cows," the women engaged in a quid pro quo slavery that served as their only vehicle to the everlasting kingdom.

Jean Rio Baker would have been considered a prime candidate for "spiritual wifery." As an older woman—just over forty—and a wealthy woman in her own right, she would have attracted the attention of any number of practicing polygamists, including Brigham Young himself. Young alone had the power to grant a man the privilege of taking another wife, so any consideration of such an arrangement would have rested with the prophet. "Out of this matter," a firsthand observer of the policy wrote in 1852, "grows an immense power based upon his knowledge of all the domestic relations in the colony; such delicate confidence begets a reverence and fear."

How Jean Rio retained her staunch independence in this climate is an enduring mystery, but perhaps it may be explained in part by the manhood of her oldest son, Walter, who might have been expected to oversee her interests. According to doctrine, her deceased husband, Henry, would "resurrect" her upon her death, claiming her as his own in the afterlife, so she would not have felt the necessity to cleave unto another man for her personal exaltation—if indeed she ever believed in that—nor would a male Saint be compelled to marry her to provide her with eternal salvation.

Now Brigham Young, who routinely gave orders relating to the domestic situations of his Saints, directed Jean Rio to immediately relocate from the relatively urban and sophisticated Salt Lake City to a remote and uncivilized outlying area.

Perhaps she was being punished as a recalcitrant or outspoken Saint. Her independent streak and intelligence could not have been repressed indefinitely.

"I have just returned from a little journey of 40 miles to a place called Ogden where I have purchased 20 acres of land," Jean Rio wrote in her diary on November 4, 1851. Directed by Young to go forth and settle far-flung communities, the Saints encroached into remote locales to expand the Kingdom of God. "I am to have a small house built during the winter, and in the spring the younger boys and myself will go there and commence farming. Walter's family, with Uncle and Aunt [Jeremiah and Mary Ann Bateman], will remain in my home in Salt Lake City." (Walter; his English wife, Eliza; and their infant son would eventually join Jean Rio in Ogden.) With her usual enthusiasm and optimism, she embraced the potential. "I was shown several specimens of the produce of the country, and took home with me a pumpkin weighing 53 pounds, but I saw some weighing 90 pounds, also potatoes of three pounds."

So it was that she pledged to take up farming, relying solely on sixteen-year-old William and twelve-year old Charles Edward to help her. The younger three—Elizabeth, John, and Charles West—were age ten and under, and could not have been expected to contribute much in the way of labor, committed as Jean Rio was to home-schooling them as well. What she thought and felt of this destiny in Zion is markedly absent from her contemporaneous diary—did she avoid committing her true feelings to paper for fear her diary would be discovered by others?—though made abundantly clear decades later.

As her new home was under construction in Ogden she

spent her first Christmas in Salt Lake City. "A delightful day ushered in not by the ringing of bells, as our city does not possess any, but by the firing of cannons," she wrote. For two hours at daybreak Captain Pitt's Brass Band, an ensemble of English converts, serenaded the city. At ten a.m. she attended the formal festivities. "The Governor with several members of the Legislature were present with their Ladies."

This would be the last joyous celebration she would record in Utah.

> MARCH 22, 1852. Removed to Ogden, accompanied by my
> son William and the younger children. Now I suppose I have
> finished my ramblings for my whole life.

If the surviving diary is an accurate indication, Jean Rio Baker now laid down her pen. Her next entry—at least in this diary—would be seventeen years later. Her life in Utah would be one of failed promise, perpetual disappointment, and ultimate poverty as the church to which she had been so thoroughly devoted appropriated her fortune. It was "a life so unremittingly tough, demanding, frustrating, burdensome," as Robert Coles writes of the frontier existence. Women like Jean Rio left England for Utah in search of an exalted life. But what she, like thousands of others, found was a reality Coles describes as "hunger, sickness, the loss of loved ones, and day in, day out, a seemingly endless expanse of backbreaking toil, with no sign that even a modest good fortune was forthcoming."

Her new village, formally laid out by Young, sprawled between the forks of the Ogden and the Weber rivers. There she did her best to remain faithful—or at least to appear so—joining in community and church affairs, acting in early stage productions, and tending to her family and the daily dramas of child rearing under the most primitive frontier America conditions. She was the first to lead the congregational singing in the Ogden church, with her son William playing violin. Though the first years on her farm were fruitful, by 1853 external influences were causing fear and paranoia in Zion.

Several "Gentile" federal officials appointed by President Fillmore to preside in Utah Territory had arrived during the summer of 1851, just weeks before Jean Rio got there. They were greeted with derision and threats. These federal agents had quickly returned to Washington, D.C., with tales of the Mormons' anti-American sentiments and strange practices that alarmed the president and Congress. Reporting that polygamy was practiced widely, that a well-trained and well-armed Mormon militia routinely murdered dissidents, and that the entire territory was riddled with sedition, these "runaway officials," as the Mormons called them, presented an unsettling portrait.

Coinciding with this testimony, Lt. John Williams Gunnison, a brilliant U.S. Army officer, wrote a best-selling book about the Mormon experiment in the Rocky Mountains. Assigned to survey the land between the thirty-eighth and thirty-ninth parallels for a transcontinental railroad—a prospect Brigham Young regarded with enmity—Gunnison had wintered in Salt Lake City. During that time he undertook to write a study of the people and their religion. *The Mormons, or Latter-Day Saints, in the Valley of the Great Salt Lake: A History of Their Rise and Progress, Peculiar Doctrines, Present Condition, and Prospects, Derived from Personal Observation, During a Residence Among Them* was published in 1852 to a shocked national audience, and it prompted a congressional debate on the rebellious territory.

Gunnison's revelations confirmed the federal officials' claims that polygamy was indeed pervasive, inciting Young to proclaim publicly for the first time that "the Principle" was divinely inspired. The doctrine emerged into national awareness just as "the transformation of the home into an affective, sentimental nest was elevating monogamy to a near religion," writes a scholar of the movement. "The presumed superiority of Western culture was closely related, it was believed, to its sexual ethic." Flouting the sacred institution of marriage, Young had handed his enemies a sword. Northern congressmen drew an analogy to slavery, moving the subject of Utah Territory into the limelight. The inchoate Republican Party now referred to polygamy and slavery in its platform, vowing to eradicate these twin relics of barbarism. Young thought both institutions divine, once telling *New York Tribune* editor Horace Greeley that slavery should not be abolished until "the curse pronounced on Ham" was removed. Young found scriptural support for both, and he believed that the men in his utopian society were entitled to as many slaves as Abraham and as many wives as Solomon. Young saw polygamy as a cornerstone of an advanced civilization, believing that society's ills found their root in the subjugation of the male's sexual needs. Fostered by the notion that men possessed a greater

Brigham Young with some of his wives and children in his Salt Lake City mansion a few years after Jean Rio first met him.

sexual drive than women—along with the entrenched opinion that women were inferior—the doctrine faulted monogamy for wasting sperm. In a religion in which populating the afterlife was paramount, such "waste" was a sin.

As federal legislators sought a solution to the problem, Jean Rio struggled to raise a crop in harsh soil. The daily challenge of feeding her family became paramount. While political tensions escalated, crop failures and drought added to her burden. In 1853 she buried her youngest son, Charles West, who had been kicked by a horse in one of those gruesome if commonplace frontier accidents—more evidence to her of the frailty and uncertainty of American life. The remaining children became more useful as they grew, but the land was unforgiving. "This little family of Londoners," one account described them, "knowing nothing of agriculture, trying to make a living on a little patch of worthless land."

Still, the hardship could not erode Jean Rio's essential goodness. Every starving Indian, tramp, or displaced "Gentile" seemed to find his way to her kitchen, where generosity prevailed. Her home, though increasingly barren, remained a place where friends, relatives, and neighbors all gathered; her high-spirited and curious mind was seductive and comforting in hard times. Meager as the meals became, she always took afternoon tea and set a formal table for dinner with what fine china survived. Music was a mainstay in all of the Baker homes—hers as well as those of her grown children—with most of her offspring renowned for their singing, instrument playing, or theatrical performing, or all three. All her grown sons had reputations for showing tenderness in a harsh environment. "The Baker men were known particularly for never whipping a child," wrote an early pioneer; such a reputation was unusual for the period and place, where "a lot of men unmercifully beat their children and horses." A love of children and dogs, of laughter and dramatics set the family apart from the more dour and pious neighbors.

Jean Rio rose to the challenge in these times of trial, just as she had done while leading her family across the ocean and plains. She was called upon to deliver babies, to prepare bodies for quick burial, and to attend the sick, and along the way she cultivated her aptitude as a medicine woman of sorts. Her collection of roots and herbs expanded, her quick mind naturally grasping the healing powers of plants. By necessity, the bejeweled pianist and singer had evolved into a botanist, a midwife, an undertaker, and a nurse.

With the theocracy now starved for cash, faced as it was with the burgeoning financial demands of building up a military for what seemed like an inevitable clash with the U.S. Army, Brigham Young instituted new rules of stewardship. In 1854 Jean Rio was required to convey all of her property, including cash and goods as well as her beloved piano, to Young as "Trustee in Trust" of the church. She could remain in her home and cultivate her land only so long as she was deemed a faithful servant. (Some accounts indicate she had traded the piano to Young earlier for wheat to feed her hungry family.) The piano wound up in Amelia Palace, the home of Young's favorite wife, a beautiful Englishwoman named Ann Eliza Webb Dee Young Denning, who would ultimately scandalize him and the church by filing for divorce and giving lectures nationwide critical of Mormonism.

A fresh wave of fanaticism permeated Zion in 1856. Disaffection and widespread apostasy—brought on by a combination of unrelenting poverty, unhappiness with the daily reality of polygamy, and whisperings of blood-atonement murders—threatened the stability of the church and Young's despotic sway. That year a swarm of locusts—what would become known as the "Mormon cricket"—decimated the fields of Deseret, leading to a famine of devastating proportions. Collective morale plummeted, and Saints began to abandon their barren farms, setting their sights on newly settled California.

Jean Rio's piano was dismantled and crated, its crate dipped in tar to weatherproof it for ocean and river crossings. The inlaid Collard & Collard square grand was the first piano brought by wagon train into the intermountain West—a rare treasure. The Mormon prophet Brigham Young acquired her beloved instrument after the once-wealthy Jean Rio had been reduced to poverty. It is now on display in the Mormon Temple Museum in Salt Lake City.

A move to California became synonymous with apostasy to those who remained loyal to Young, and those who fled did so in darkness and secrecy and with justified fear of swift and cruel retribution.

Meanwhile, Young's plan to transport thousands of poor Scandinavian converts across the plains was producing tragic results. In the early years of emigration, the church's Perpetual

Emigrating Fund had advanced money to European converts to make the journey to Salt Lake City—money that Jean Rio never had to use. The emigrants were obligated to repay the money at 10 percent interest once they arrived in Zion or in goods if they had no cash. But now Young announced that the church could no longer "afford to purchase wagons and teams as in times past." He was, he said, "thrown back upon my old plan—to make handcarts, and let the emigration foot it." That idea led to the greatest disaster in the history of western migration, exceeding by seven times the lives lost in the Donner-party tragedy a decade earlier.

In what he said was a divinely inspired invention, Young conceived of a contraption, called a handcart, fashioned after those used by porters in New York City railroad stations. The lightweight handcarts were hastily constructed from unseasoned wood, measured the same width as a wagon, and had a handle like that of a wheelbarrow by which to be pulled or pushed. Five people were assigned to each cart, which was laden with their belongings; each emigrant was allowed to bring seventeen pounds of baggage that included clothing and bedding. For the sake of economy the wheels had no tires—a factor that would lead to many breakdowns. Insufficiently rationed, many emigrants starved as they endured frostbite during early snows on the plains. "With a morsel of bread or biscuit in their hands, nearing it to their mouths, could be seen men, hale-looking and apparently strong, stiff in death," wrote a witness. The ill-conceived plan led to the deaths of sixty-seven in one blizzard alone. Many of those who died had been handicapped; they had been lured to Zion by missionaries promising safe passage and free land. Most Mormons at Salt Lake held Young personally responsible.

Fearing that his flock had become less zealous, Young ushered in the "Mormon Reformation"—a terrifying period church historians later referred to as the "Reign of Terror"—during which loyalist enforcers interrogated the settlers. Encouraging Saints to inform on their neighbors, family, and friends who were weak in the faith, Young's "Avenging Angels," or Danites—originally named the Sons of Dan by Joseph Smith for the man described in the Bible's Book of Judges—were the enforcement arm of the prophet. A secret police that brought swift retribution to apostates and to antagonistic "Gentiles," they were the elite unit of Young's "Army of Israel." "Backsliders were to be hewn down," according to writer Josiah Gibbs. Young declared so in increasingly fiery sermons, verbally attacking the apathy or outright defection that undermined the urgent task of building his "Biblical City of Zion." During the winter of 1856–1857 church elders swept through the Mormons' homes, demanding that everyone be rebaptized and forcing church members to answer fourteen questions:

1. Have you shed innocent blood or assented thereto?

2. Have you committed adultery?

3. Have you betrayed your brother?

4. Have you borne false witness against your neighbor?

5. Do you get drunk?

6. Have you stolen?

7. Have you lied?

8. Have you contracted debts without prospect of paying?

9. Have you labored faithfully for your wage?
10. Have you coveted that which belongs to another?
11. Have you taken the name of the Lord in vain?
12. Do you preside in your family as a servant of God?
13. Have you paid your tithing in all things?
14. Do you wash your bodies once a week?

If Saints admitted to laxity, or if their neighbors testified against them, they were required to renew their commitment to the faith, endure various forms of penance, and vow allegiance to the prophet. Untold numbers tried to leave the territory, mostly in vain, as the religious extremists gained dominance.

During the "Reformation," Young preached inflammatory sermons about adultery and apostasy, transgressions so grave, in his eyes, that they could be cleansed only by slitting the throats of the sinners from ear to ear. "There are sins that can be atoned for by an offering upon an altar as in ancient days," he thundered in one such speech. "And there are sins that the blood of a lamb, or a calf, or of turtle doves, cannot remit, but they must be atoned for by the blood of the man." Openly embracing the doctrine that had been concealed since the earliest days of the church, Young sent panic into his followers and outrage into the nation at large.

In March 1857 the prophet began to escalate his rhetoric against the U.S. government. Railing against America, he issued a defiant proclamation in July 1857 that his government in Utah, and only his government, would decide which laws would be enforced in the territory. President James Buchanan considered Young's posturing treasonous, and he made armed

A young Brigham Young in the
summer of 1857, a few months
before the Mountain Meadows
Massacre and in the midst of his
defiance of federal authority in the
so-called Utah War.

intervention in Utah a priority for his new administration.
That spring and summer Buchanan appointed three new federal judges, a U.S. marshal, and a superintendent of Indian
affairs to be installed in the territory. They would be accompanied by more than twenty-five hundred troops under the
command of Brigadier General William Harney. In announcing his action to Congress, Buchanan claimed it was his duty
to restore the supremacy of the Constitution and laws.

While awaiting the "invasion" by the U.S. Army, Young
exhorted his followers, already intimidated by the "Reforma-

tion," to prepare to avenge the blood of the prophet Joseph Smith or to face violence themselves. Then, on September 7, 1857, the Mormon militia attacked a wagon train of "Gentiles" passing through Utah laden with gold. During a brutal five-day siege, the Mormons shot approximately 140 people, slitting the throats of the dead so that their blood would be returned to the earth in accordance with the doctrine of "blood atonement." The victims, mostly women and children, were slaughtered despite a pledge of safe passage.

Like many of her fellow Saints, Jean Rio was horrified upon learning the whispered details of the Mountain Meadows Massacre—an act of religious fanaticism unparalleled in American history. That Brigham Young bore significant responsibility for the crime—both before the event and in the ex post facto attempt falsely to lay responsibility on the Paiute Indians—undermined her faith not only in the religion itself, but also in the grandiose and corrupt leader. Her later descendants would point to the massacre as a decisive factor in her breach with the church. Though the church-owned *Deseret News* did not report the atrocity, rumors whipped through the entire territory. Among the most terrifying reports were stories of the fate of apostate Mormons who had joined the wagon train, hoping to accompany it safely to California. The stories that were inevitably spread by and among those who had known them, the accounts of their brutal murder at the hands of their fellow Saints—zealots committing "blood atonement"—were shocking if not incomprehensible to the faithful. There were also numerous and moving stories of Mormon men who had refused to participate in the wholesale

murder of civilians. The crime inspired widespread defections, though it was nearly impossible to leave the territory
safely. That Jean Rio did not write of the event was typical of
the moment; it was the most dangerous time imaginable for a
disillusioned Saint to confide her thoughts, even to a private
diary, and like thousands of like-minded Mormons she would
carry the shame and secret throughout the rest of her life.

At least three of her sons—Walter, William, and Charles
Edward—had been, by requirement, members of Young's military force, the Nauvoo Legion, which drilled regularly at the
tabernacle in Ogden. While there is no direct evidence that
they participated in the atrocity, which occurred more than
250 miles south of Salt Lake City, the young Baker men would
have had firsthand information from their fellow militiamen
about the killings. "The whole United States rang with its horrors," Mark Twain later wrote of the event.

As the U.S. Army marched toward Utah, Young imposed
martial law and issued a proclamation: "We intend to desolate
the Territory and conceal our families, stock, and all our
effects in the fastnesses of the mountains, where they will be
safe, while the men waylay our enemies, attack them from
ambush, stampede their animals, take the supply trains, cut
off detachments, and parties sent to canyons for wood, or on
other service." He ordered all non-Mormons to leave the territory, and he commanded all Saints to take three years' supply
of food and disappear into the wilderness rather than succumb to a federal military force camped near their city. Able-
bodied men between the ages of eighteen and forty-five were
organized into military units and the officers were ordered to

be in readiness to march to any part of the territory on short notice. "I am your leader, Latter Day Saints," he told them, "and you must follow me; and if you do not follow me you may expect that I shall go my way and you may take yours if you please." Any Mormon who defied the proclamation would be put to death, he announced.

More than twenty thousand Mormons left Salt Lake City and the nearby communities, some one hundred men staying behind to torch the abandoned fields and homes as soon as the army entered the valley. Poor and now homeless, the ragged Saints obeyed, turning their backs on all they had struggled to build. In June 1858 Young, facing defeat and humiliation, reluctantly agreed to be replaced as territorial governor and to allow federal troops to occupy Salt Lake City. The soldiers marched in order through the city's deserted streets. On July 4 Young called the refugees home. But many had exhausted their resources in the "Move South," as it was called, and were forced—or chose—to remain in the temporary settlements and begin anew.

Jean Rio was fortunate in that she was able to return to the crude dugout she had constructed in Ogden, but her future held little promise. "The famine of the year '57 and the move south in '58 are matters of history," she wrote later. "I need not say that I passed them both, and a bitter experience it was." No longer enamored with or even trusting the church, she now began to regret deeply the fateful choice she had made nearly a decade earlier, feeling she had been lured to a sinister "kingdom" under false pretenses by prevaricating missionaries. Still, as she lost her faith in Young as a divinely inspired prophet, and in the Church of Latter-day Saints as pure Christianity restored on earth, she fell back on her innate spirituality and strengthened her belief in God. Young had turned out to be the very bogus, betraying intermediary between God and the individual that Joseph Smith had warned against, and Jean Rio, like many of her fellow Mormons of the time, began to see the current church as an irremediable corruption of Smith's inspired institution.

Though her home had not been disturbed, there had been no crops sown during the summer, so the following winter was one of severe hunger. Jean Rio, like all the other women in her community, spent hours bent over a washboard, perspiring over hot irons, sewing by candlelight, or tilling the scorched earth, her genteel past fading into a distant memory. Nothing was an equalizer like pioneer life.

Soon afterward her sons Charles Edward and John, now twenty-one and seventeen years old respectively, fled Zion. Jean Rio encouraged them, though the plans for escape were of necessity kept secret from all neighbors, friends, and acquaintances, and especially from their fundamentalist brother, William. Anguished at their going, she thought of joining them, but she kept no written record of her feelings at the time—so dangerous would it have been for her if her apostasy had been uncovered. In any case, church leaders would view her with suspicion as soon as knowledge of her sons' flight became apparent, and would grill her incessantly about her own depth of conviction.

"The brothers sneaked away from Utah in the middle of the night on two horses," according to a descendant of one of the men. They would tell their future children that they knew if they were caught departing the territory they would be put to death. "Brigham Young didn't like people leaving, especially if they took horses." After a harrowing journey over the Sierra Nevada mountain range they arrived safely in San Francisco. "They could not stand poverty any longer so ran away from it," wrote their mother. She considered accompanying them to California but found herself torn between the misery of the life she knew and the unknown of yet another frontier. She had set out for "the city in the tops of the mountains" with seven children as part of what one historian has called "a pageant of divine destiny." Now, some nine years later, two sons were dead and two sons had struck out on their own to the edge of America.

"My 20-acre farm turned out to be a mere salaratus patch, killing the seed which was sown instead of producing a crop," Jean Rio recalled years later, writing an addendum to her diary. Admitting defeat, she deserted her land, moving into a "small log house" in Ogden City to learn dressmaking. "I have tried to do my best in the various circumstances in which I have been placed," she wrote. "I came here in obedience to what I believed to be a revelation of the most high God, trusting in the assurance of the Missionaries whom I believed to have the spirit of truth. I left my home, sacrificed my property, broke up every dear association, and what was and is yet dearer than all, left my beloved native land. And for what? A bubble that has burst in my grasp. It has been a severe lesson, but I can say it has led me to lean more on my Heavenly Father and less on the words of men."

CHAPTER EIGHT

Through the Veil

W ITH A GENIUS for colonizing unmatched in the annals of the West, Young had methodically expanded his domain throughout the 1850s. The English converts had included mostly laborers and stonemasons; the Americans were primarily farmers. But Young needed weavers, tailors, shoemakers, and watchmakers to build a civilized society in such isolation, and he turned to Scandinavia, Scotland, and Wales to help fill that need. To cultivate the arid land and forge tools and implements he needed more farmers and mechanics. So he shrewdly turned his attention to Denmark, a country where most men labored under aristocratic landowners and where sectarian schisms were destroying the once-solid Lutheran unity. As Young also knew, virtually all Danish adults were literate, and all the men served six years in the Danish army, which would have prepared them well for the demands of building the "City of God."

Young had sent missionaries to Denmark to preach God's command to gather in Zion, where the finest land could be had merely for the price of a survey. To become lords of the soil was a powerful, irresistible argument to the peasantry of

Denmark at a time when their prospects of owning land were nil. The plea of the missionaries to leave the Old World and its troubles for something wholly new and exhilarating was even more effective than Young had anticipated. The highly educated, exceedingly healthy, and unusually skilled Danes, donning their fine homespun clothes, wooden shoes, and woolen socks, migrated to Zion in droves, the Danish women no less courageous or enthusiastic than the men. "The monotony of a man's life was as nothing compared to a woman's," writes Icelandic author Halldór Laxness in describing the mundane gloom of Scandinavian existence at the time. Thousands of new converts would make their way to Utah. "The Danes, proverbially reluctant to sail out farther than they could row back, and traditionally considered poor pioneers," writes a historian of the movement, "nevertheless, as Mormons, left their homeland in years of actual prosperity to become hardy grass-roots settlers."

Nicolena Bertelsen, a young Danish girl, would be swept up in this fervor. Her destiny to become a plural wife—and Jean Rio Baker's daughter-in-law—thousands of miles away in a foreign land was utterly devoid of free will. Born in Denmark on January 26, 1845, Nicolena was the seventh child of Niels and Maren Bertelsen. The Bertelsen family home was a white cottage on the moorland where Niels tilled the rolling heath for the wealthy landlord who lived in a manor house nearby. Though farming and fishing were his mainstays, Niels also hunted swans. Maren would pluck the soft down from the birds' breasts to make pillows and comforters for their ten children.

Comprising the Jutland Peninsula and hundreds of mostly uninhabited islands, Denmark was a small dominion of northern Europe surrounded by water except at Jutland's forty-two-mile border with Germany. With its blue lakes and white coastlines, the sea-level landscape was home to some of history's more savage people. From the ancient Cimbri and Teutons who raided Europe to the later Vikings—fierce pirates and warriors who terrorized England, Ireland, Germany, France, and Russia for three hundred years—the Danes were notoriously courageous and cruel. By the fifteenth century, the once heavily forested land was completely denuded at the behest of kings seeking timber for Danish ships. The ravaged expanse acquired a sad emptiness, dotted as it was with windmills, thatched roofs, and massive stone castles.

But the nineteenth-century Denmark of the Bertelsens was known more for the gentle fairy tales of Hans Christian Andersen and the existentialist philosophy of Søren Kierkegaard than for the brutality of its past. Having lost Norway to Sweden in 1814 during the Napoleonic wars, Denmark had fallen into a thirty-year depression, only to emerge as a European capital of art and literature. Its radical educational reform—designed to prepare the peasant for his struggle in political and economic life—required that every boy and girl between the ages of six and fourteen attend school. This system of compulsory education for all was the most advanced in the world, ushering in Denmark's golden age and having far-reaching consequences for communities in the American West settled by Danes.

Niels and Maren were typical of their time and place,

exhibiting nothing of the religious fundamentalism that would define their midlife years. Though Maren was—like 97 percent of the Danish population—an orthodox Lutheran, Niels preferred the almanac to the Bible and relentlessly teased his wife about her piety. But when Mormon missionaries reached the Bertelsens' tiny village of Staarup in 1852—three years after Jean Rio Baker and her husband were converted in England—Maren was an eager convert to their message of hope and fulfillment. "In Scandinavia, Zion was proclaimed in a vigorous literature ranging from the sober and moralizing to the extravagant and apocalyptic that sometimes failed to distinguish between Zion as metaphor," according to a scholar of Scandinavian immigration, " . . . identifying Deseret with Zion of the Psalms." Whether allegory or reality, the missionaries portrayed America as the land of promise where the most optimistic dreams could be realized. At the heart of the Mormon movement was the "gathering" of converts to Zion, where "they would never know themselves otherwise than saints." The serious-minded Maren was convinced after only one meeting with the missionaries, while Niels remained reluctant. But when their landlord evicted them from their home of twenty-one years for hosting the Mormons, Niels was so outraged by the injustice that he too joined the faith. In 1853 the entire Bertelsen family was baptized in haste and secrecy and the children began departing one by one for the new Zion.

Nicolena was the fourth child to leave Denmark, entrusted to the care of two missionaries returning to Utah. That November, the blue-eyed eight-year-old swathed in bulky warm clothing, a peasant handkerchief tied over her yellow curls, waited on a busy wharf. Arm in arm with her playmate and sister Ottomina, who would stay behind, she stood clutching a bundle of belongings. Terrified at the reality of the solo journey and mystified by the talk of "salvation" and "Zion," she felt helpless to challenge her parents.

Nicolena had tearfully begged her mother to let her take her favorite doll, but the stern Maren refused, saying only necessities could be taken—a denial Nicolena remembered her entire life. She watched the deck crews, wishing that her parents would suddenly change their minds. Instead, Maren told her to be a good girl and to pray. Stuffing a small Bible into her armload, Maren directed her to read from it every day. "Keep clean," Nicolena remembered her mother telling her. "And wait on yourself, never be a burden to anyone. And never, never cry!"

Her childhood had been blissfully happy and she could not understand why her parents would want to change any of it. She loved going out with her father in the fishing boat as he hunted the wild birds and then making miniature down comforters for her dolls. She and Ottomina, so close in age, romped through the meadows after completing their chores, "digging in the sandy beaches, playing under the leafy boughs of the beech trees," she would later recall.

Ottomina had saved her pennies to buy sweetcakes for Nicolena, and she now pressed them into her sister's hand. Nicolena quickly brushed her tears away so her mother could not see. She later recalled that she had no appetite then, or for many weeks later, and the sweetcakes went uneaten.

Similar to Jean Rio before her, she spent three stormy

months on the Atlantic Ocean. She was seasick and homesick, nauseated from the ship's fare and unable to sleep on the hard beds. A fire on the boat threatened the entire company and a second ship responded to their distress signal, rescuing all on board. The ship docked in New York, and the spectacle of the city was unlike anything in Nicolena's rural homeland. Lonely and miserable, Nicolena continued by rail to Chicago, and then on to St. Louis. She arrived in St. Louis in March 1854, having traveled by sea and land for four months. There, to her horror, the missionaries told her they could take her no farther. They turned her over to an employment agency and promised to inform her family of her whereabouts. Speaking only Danish and possessing no money, Nicolena was so overtaken with fear and despair that she would later reflect that all the trials she thenceforth endured paled in comparison.

Months passed with no word from Denmark or Utah. A wealthy family offered her a position as a babysitter, a job she would hold for two years. Though the family was kind and loving, teaching her English and offering her a permanent home with them, Nicolena maintained a single-minded determination to join other family members who had already made the voyage to Zion. She saved every cent she earned until she had enough to buy transportation on a Mississippi steamboat from St. Louis to Council Bluffs, which, she had been told, was the starting point for wagon trains heading to Utah.

Now ten years old and venturing alone into an unknown world, Nicolena found a handcart company assembling for the long trek west. But there was no place for a young girl without a family to watch over her. Touched by the Danish girl's predicament, an emigrant offered to let her travel with his family in exchange for help with his pregnant wife. By this time, Nicolena's emotional pain had healed and with a bit of maturity her fears had abated. She faced the journey with excitement, and later in life recalled the experience as "a glorious adventure" marred only by one terrifying episode. Once, when the company stopped for wagon repairs, an exhausted Nicolena fell asleep in a willow grove on the bank of a stream. She awakened to find herself alone, the handcart train so far ahead it was no longer visible. Crying and screaming, she began running on the prairie, following the train's tracks. Suddenly she saw a horseman galloping toward her, and she assumed that he was an Indian warrior. Instead he was her rescuer—the rear guard of the company who had noticed she was missing. The guard lifted the girl onto the horse and calmed her. Convinced that her prayers had been answered, that divine intervention had plucked her from harm, she felt her first stirrings of faith. Perhaps her parents had been right, that God indeed would usher true believers to safety in the "city in the tops of the mountains." In retrospect, the journey was idealized in her mind. "She was, after all, a child with a child's natural happy outlook," one of her daughters later recalled. "During the long trek west, the great outdoors, the lure of unaccustomed scenes and activities, and the knowledge that at last she was on her way to Zion made it almost entirely a glorious adventure."

Nicolena thought it miraculous when she was reunited with her brother Lars and sister Letty, who had arrived before her and were settled in the south-central Utah community of

Richfield. Letty oversaw Nicolena's adolescence, helping her improve her English and continuing what Nicolena called her "book learning." An eager student, Nicolena became proficient in the common pioneer pursuits of cleaning, combing, and spinning the raw wool from sheep, and weaving, dyeing, and sewing the cloth. "A lovely blonde with luxuriant honey-colored hair of the texture of spun silk," as one account described her, she had a unique sense of style perhaps acquired from her years in cosmopolitan St. Louis. She became a talented seamstress and by the time she was fourteen years old was able to support herself as a dressmaker. "Good taste in her own dress and an inborn genius at sewing soon earned for her a reputation, from which she was able to earn many a dollar," according to one account. In her spare time, she would join other young people in the wheat fields, spending hours at a time gathering the choice grasses. Resourceful and ingenious, she then braided wheat straw into plaits with which she decorated bonnets, and she sold the bonnets to the more affluent of the Saints.

At the age of nineteen she fell in love with a fellow Dane named Christian Christensen. But on April 21, 1866, Christensen was mortally wounded in an Indian uprising near Marysvale, Utah. Nicolena cared for him for six weeks and insisted on a deathbed wedding. Being "sealed" to him "for time and eternity" meant, according to Mormon doctrine, that she and any future children she bore would belong to him in the "hereafter." Their love story became the subject of a ballad sung throughout Utah over the next century.

Grief-stricken upon her husband's death, Nicolena took a

Jean Rio's daughter-in-law, Nicolena Bertelsen Baker, as a ten-year-old girl walked the entire way from what is now Council Bluffs, Iowa, to Salt Lake City. The second wife in a polygamous marriage to Jean Rio's son William George Baker, she raised her family of ten children in near-abject poverty in the frontier settlement of Richfield, Utah.

job as a maid at the Richfield House hotel, owned by the well-to-do Englishman William George Baker and his wife, Hannah. The second-oldest son of Jean Rio, William had helped his mother farm in Ogden until Brigham Young ordered him to go south to help settle the community of Moroni in 1862, and then Richfield the following year. He was one of thirty-nine men chosen by Young to locate areas in Deseret that would sustain a growing Mormon population. The only son of Jean Rio's to remain a practicing Mormon, he had been well rewarded by Brigham Young for his dedication. In addition to being a teacher and businessman, he held the lucrative patronage contract with the U.S. government to deliver mail in Utah Territory, ran a stagecoach line from Nephi to Panguitch, and practiced law. As the first settler in Richfield he set up a civil rather than a theocratic government.

William, though married and already the father of five, was instantly smitten by Nicolena's "unusual fresh beauty," as he put it. A believer in "the Principle," he appealed to Young for permission to take her as his second wife.

Like most women in her situation in post-"Reformation" Utah, Jean Rio was extremely cautious in expressing strong opposition to Mormon practices, including that of polygamy. She would almost certainly have known Fanny Stenhouse, an educated English convert like herself, who was beginning to voice the opinion that polygamy was the "worst oppression and degradation of woman ever known in a civilized country." Stenhouse—whose husband, journalist T.B.H. Stenhouse, had publicly and sensationally abandoned polygamy—came to the attention of Harriet Beecher Stowe, author of the novel *Uncle Tom's Cabin*, about the progress from slavery to freedom. Stowe was encouraging both Stenhouses to write about their Mormon experience, and while it would be a few more years before each of them published a book, the couple became the core of a dissident group of Utah intellectuals. In the run-up to the Civil War, as the Republican Party likened polygamy to slavery, a national eye was turned toward Utah, and Jean Rio observed the situation with a keen curiosity.

For the sake of family harmony, Jean Rio put her disapproval aside and embraced her new daughter-in-law with compassion and empathy. While she might have tried to dissuade her son from practicing polygamy, she knew that the young Nicolena had little, if any, say in the matter.

Indeed, the young Danish woman found herself suddenly "sealed" to William. Despite her objection, her marriage to the beloved Christensen was "set aside" by Brigham Young, and thus her only avenue "through the veil" and to eternal salvation now rested with William Baker. "Even though Lena may not have been in love with him at the time," according to one account, "she realized it was the natural and dutiful thing for a girl to marry a good man and do her part toward the common good." She confided her true feelings to her sister Ottomina, and stoically determined not to complain. If anything, her faith in God and devotion to her church became stronger, as she chose to see her misfortunes as evidence of God's love. She vowed that she would cultivate love for this older husband, a tall man with curly black hair and striking blue eyes who made every effort at tenderness with her. "She was the type of girl who hungered and thirsted for knowledge, culture, and beauty," according to a Mormon historian. "William filled that need. He was ever kind, considerate, and gallant despite the difficulties of celestial marriage."

Her "bride's nest," according to one account, was "a primitive adobe dugout" in close proximity and stark contrast to Hannah's relatively comfortable log home. Nine months after marrying William, Nicolena gave birth to a baby girl, whom she christened Ottomina after her favorite sister. Over the next decades she would often be pregnant and almost always destitute, eventually bearing ten children who were not legitimate by civil standards. She would spend her life in a crude shanty in the shadow of the more honored "first family," her own babies pitted for survival against William's thirteen children by Hannah. Still, Nicolena brought beauty to the harshest environment. She "made her little home so clean and cozily beautiful that it became a saying in the village that 'Lena's house,' whether it was a dugout or a two-story dwelling, always looked like a palace," according to one account. "She was the very soul of orderliness, system, and neatness in her person and in her housekeeping." As her sons grew, they hauled the winter's wood for her, cut and baled alfalfa for her livestock, while also supporting her with the income they earned driving the stagecoach that brought the mail to the mining camps of Nevada. The younger children helped with the cows and chickens, the garden, and the fruit orchard.

"The little happinesses, the large griefs, the moves from town to town, the uncertainties of life as a second wife, the sorrows and ecstasies of mothering and rearing ten children, poverty, sickness, and death," as one history described Nicolena's years of marriage, were typical for a woman of her time and place. What carried her through, by all accounts, was a keen and infectious streak of humor.

By 1864, Jean Rio found herself in increasing conflict with her polygamist son William, their relationship strained by his extreme religious beliefs and his attempts to control her financial affairs. As in civil war, such family divisions were heartbreaking—a toll of the parting of the once faithful. She had begun to lose faith not long after her arrival in Salt Lake City and had now suffered a series of serious blows—the reality of polygamy; the fact that women were denied a role in the church's hierarchy; the authoritarian, dictatorial patriarchy of Brigham Young; the horrendous Mountain Meadows Massacre; the church's turning a blind eye to her poverty; even the expropriation of the piano she had brought across an ocean and a continent. Jean Rio of all people knew that rejecting the church openly was not a choice if she was to remain in Utah. In that theocratic society there was hatred and shunning, cleaving mothers from sons, wives from husbands, brothers from sisters, with the apostates branded as if they were the lepers of biblical times. She had received her "endowments" a year after her arrival in Utah—a ceremony that required a strong commitment—but by 1857, if not earlier, Jean Rio had left the fold and was considering her own life's options, with her eye on California.

Like her new daughter-in-law, Nicolena, she had had her share of brief but blissful romance. In 1864, to the dismay of William, she had married a "Gentile" named Edward Pearce— one of the relatively few non-Mormons living among the Saints. "I had been a widow fifteen years, my children all married, and I felt I had the right to decide for myself in a matter that only concerned myself," she wrote. At the age of fifty-four, she had found a happiness that had eluded her since her arrival in Zion. "I hoped that my old age would have been cheered by his companionship—that I should no longer be alone," she wrote near the end of her life, adding it to her original diary. "But it was not to be. He only lived six months. That time was of unbroken peace and comfort, and his sudden death was a severe blow to me. Perhaps I was not worthy of being the wife of so good a man, for he certainly was one in whom there was no guile."

That year too, the devout William was "disfellowshipped" by the church for purchasing a pair of boots from a "Gentile" merchant, though he was later reinstated. Jean Rio's son Walter, along with his wife, Eliza, and their many children, was planning to join his brothers John and Charles in California, where they were prospering as merchants and politicians. Her two remaining children in Utah were busy raising their own families: Elizabeth had married a successful Ogden businessman, and William had little time for his mother now that he had two wives and numerous offspring. While Jean Rio had lacked the courage to join her sons in a dangerous nighttime flight by horseback years earlier, unwilling to risk pursuit by Young's "Avenging Angels," it had become easier to leave the territory in the 1860s.

The dangerous period of apostate killings had waned, as the U.S. presence in the territory made itself felt. The watchful eye of federal officials mitigated much of the frontier violence and U.S. Army escorts oversaw a burgeoning traffic of disaffected Mormons fleeing Zion. California newspapers reported that thousands of fugitive Saints were making their way west, "refugees from the Mormon kingdom who had sought the army's protection because they feared their former coreligionists," as one account described them. The flow of Mormon defectors had become the largest emigration to that point, far surpassing even the California gold rush. The U.S. Army posted advertisements directed at dissidents throughout Salt Lake City. "Having through His Excellency Governor Cumming," read one, "asked of Gen. Johnston a military escort to conduct us beyond the lines of danger, on our road to California, and the same being readily granted, we respectfully solicit all who wish to avail themselves of this security, and can be ready for an early start, to convene at the California House."

Still, at this point in her life Jean Rio, middle-aged and twice widowed, was reluctant to journey by horse and wagon to San Francisco, escort or no escort. As it happened, her "escape" from Zion came with the much-anticipated, and bitterly fought, transcontinental railroad.

"Next to winning the Civil War and abolishing slavery, building the first transcontinental railroad, from Omaha, Nebraska, to Sacramento, California, was the greatest achievement of the American people in the nineteenth century," writes Stephen E. Ambrose. The government had pitted two of the country's largest corporations—the Union Pacific and the Central Pacific—against each other in a race to link the continent, "thus ensuring an empire of liberty running from sea to shining sea." Brigham Young battled the railroad every step of the way, viewing it as a threat to his tottering realm, despite government assurances that the opening of a central route to the Pacific would benefit the sect's gathering to Zion. Young "never had taken the trouble to conceal his inflexible opposition to any attempt to build a railroad through his empire," according to historian R. Kent Fielding. Not only would the railroad bring an influx of the depraved and despised "Gentiles" to Utah Territory, Young believed, but it would also give dissatisfied Saints a ready means of retreat.

Though highly controversial, the dream of a transcontinental railroad had finally materialized on March 2, 1853, when the Thirty-second Congress appropriated $150,000 authorizing Secretary of War Jefferson Davis to establish a Bureau of Explorations and Surveys. Davis dispatched the U.S. Army Topographical Corps to map possible routes between the thirty-second and forty-ninth parallels. Among the explorers Davis selected was Captain John Williams Gunnison, published critic of the Mormons, who would survey between the thirty-eighth and thirty-ninth parallels from the Arkansas headwaters to the Great Basin, by way of the Santa Clara River in southwestern Utah. Gunnison recommended a line "crossing the North Platte into the South Pass, over the Coal Basin, skirting the Bear River Mountains at the northern base, near Bridger's fort; and through the Bear and Weber Kanyons . . . to the banks of the Valley of Lake Utah"—or into the heart of Zion. But in October of that year, Mormons along with mercenary renegade Indians massacred Gunnison and his party on the Sevier River in central Utah. Federal investigators concluded that Mormon leaders had ordered the murders in retaliation for Gunnison's exposé, as well as in an effort to stop the railroad expansion. The Gunnison tragedy, along with other depredations by the theocracy, would eventually move President James Buchanan to send troops in the so-called Utah War of 1857.

After all the surveys were completed, Jefferson Davis recommended a southern route from New Orleans to Los Angeles that would have greatly enhanced the power and wealth of the southern states. But northern, free-state politicians blocked the scheme.

The Central Pacific Railroad, owned by a bevy of wealthy and powerful California business tycoons, was formally incorporated in June 1861. The intent was to build a railroad from California across the Sierra Nevada. The following year saw the creation of the Union Pacific Railroad by New York and Chicago industrialists. That line was intended to run west from Omaha, Nebraska. The two lines were to meet at a yet-to-be-determined location near Salt Lake City. The Pacific Railway Act of 1862 had chartered the Central Pacific to build east until it joined tracks with the Union Pacific at the Nevada-Utah border. "But the wording was vague," according to historian Glenn Chesney Quiett, and the powerful Central Pacific lobbyists in Washington convinced Congress to amend the act to allow both railroads to continue construction until they met. "Just where this was to be was not stated, and since every mile of track meant thousands of dollars in subsidies, each road was anxious to build as long a line as possible," wrote Quiett. With the amended act of 1866, the race was on.

Brigham Young's position toward the railroad softened when he saw its inevitability and grasped the significance of a route that might skirt his territory. By 1863 he had become so eager for the railroad to come to Zion that he conducted his own surveys and purchased five shares of stock in Union Pacific. He began bartering for construction contracts and extracting other concessions, including a guarantee that the line would be built through Salt Lake City. Explaining his change of attitude to the Saints, he claimed he had had a vision in which "the Lord had revealed to him that the Union Pacific would build directly to Salt Lake City." California governor Leland Stanford, one of the backers of the Central Pacific, traveled to Salt Lake City five times to lobby Young on his company's behalf, but reportedly found the prophet "cold and close."

When a Union Pacific engineer, Grenville Dodge, declared that the road should instead be built north of Salt Lake City to Ogden, Young felt double-crossed. Furious, he "called the faithful together and preached a scorching sermon against this impious engineer and his railroad," according to one account. Coincident to Dodge's life being threatened in Utah was Union Pacific officials' telling Young he could "name his price and set other conditions" for a construction contract.

Young readily agreed, after meeting with his twelve apostles. He then called together his followers to reveal the new and contradictory "divine" plan. "The Lord, in another vision, had commanded the Mormons to help the Union Pacific," he was said to have announced. With that, he signed a $2 million contract "to do the Union's grading, tunneling, and bridge-building from Ogden east into the Wasatch Mountains," according to one account. Young then placed notices in the

Salt Lake City newspapers "calling on all the men who wanted work to report to three of his sons, who were ready to hire." Characteristically, Young hedged his bets, and by the project's completion Mormon graders were working feverishly at either end, with Young not only heavily invested in Union Pacific but maintaining a quarter-interest in the firm of Benson, Farr & West, a subcontracting company for Central Pacific run by three Mormon bishops.

William Baker was rewarded yet again for his many years of faithful devotion, receiving the high-salaried position of bookkeeper and secretary for one of Utah's most powerful men, Chauncey Walker West, who, with Ezra Taft Benson and Lorin Farr, had received the coveted construction contract with the Central Pacific Railroad. The race to reach Ogden took on epic proportions, as both sides were pushing with all possible speed, employing ruthless tactics. Union Pacific induced the workers of Central Pacific with higher wages, forcing Central Pacific to match the raises as well as to bring in beefy Irishmen to bolster the Chinese crews. In the final push to complete the track, Union Pacific laid seven miles of track in one day, prompting Central Pacific to claim it could lay ten miles in a day. Having made a $10,000 bet with a Union Pacific executive who believed it couldn't be done, Governor Stanford journeyed to Utah to observe the historic event firsthand. Benson, Farr & West "received more than the contract price," according to one account, "for so anxious had been the company to lengthen its line that Stanford had agreed with West, on condition that the work be pushed forward with all possible speed, to pay him whatever it might cost."

"A great feat has been accomplished today," the *San Francisco Evening Bulletin* announced. "Ten miles and fifty-eight feet of railroad . . . has been laid between daylight and sundown. The most powerful track-laying force ever mobilized of 848 men completed the task. Two million pounds of iron were handled during the day." When Stanford pounded a Nevada silver sledge into the golden spike at Promontory Summit in Utah, on May 10, 1869, joining the Central Pacific and Union Pacific tracks, Jean Rio's future opened before her.

"As luck would have it," writes one historian, "a wagon train hove into view of the Promontory crowd as the final tie was eased into place; the juxtaposition of old and new struck the celebrants as fittingly dramatic." The nation erupted in celebration, as if to symbolize the independence Jean Rio must have felt. The Liberty Bell in Philadelphia rang. San Francisco fired 220 cannons. Fireworks lit the skies in New York and Washington, and Chicago staged its largest parade of the century. Zion was no longer an isolated enclave, beholden only to the totalitarian rule of Brigham Young. It had once refused to join with America; now America had subsumed it. An easily accessible world now stretched 690 miles west across the Sierras to Sacramento and 1,086 miles east and across the Rockies to the Missouri, making freedom a sudden possibility for thousands of Saints who had long since resigned themselves to virtual captivity. Jean Rio would be among those who seized their freedom.

Ironically, the devout Mormon-bishop-turned-railroad-magnate Chauncey West would be her deliverer. West, who was among Utah's earliest pioneers, most prominent businessmen, wealthiest citizens, and avid polygamists, presided over an ostentatious estate in Ogden that covered an entire city block. Homes for each of his nine wives were graced with gardens and orchards more reminiscent to Jean Rio of her English upbringing than her Utah destitution. West was a longtime intimate of Brigham Young, serving as a general in the six-thousand-member Nauvoo Legion, or Utah Territorial Militia, during Zion's most controversial time, the year between the Mountain Meadows Massacre and the Utah War.

Though a decade younger than Jean Rio, West had become one of her closest friends. His brother Lewis was married to Jean Rio's daughter Elizabeth, and Jean Rio had adopted a maternal mien toward both West "boys." She became particularly worried about Chauncey during the summer of 1869, as he seemed ravaged by stress in the wake of the massive railroad construction project he had supervised. The tracks had been completed months before, and yet the California industrialists who owned the Central Pacific had not sent the payroll for the thousands of Mormon laborers, nor honored their commitment to pay the hundreds of thousands of dollars in fees promised to West's own three-man partnership (in which Brigham Young had a one-quarter interest). West was absorbing the pressure from increasingly hostile workers—many of whom had been recruited by William Baker—and as his anxiety increased, his health declined.

In November Chauncey West decided to travel by rail to San Francisco to meet with Stanford, who had made a personal commitment to West to fulfill the obligations, and to secure a final settlement with Central Pacific. In his weakened state he turned to Jean Rio for the nursing that had become her specialty. The proficiency she showed in caring for the injured and infirm during her wagon-train crossing had evolved over time into a nearly professional skill. She saw this as a calling to serve humankind, which to her was the Christian obligation. As her faith in Mormonism faltered, her devotion to healing the afflictions of others strengthened.

When West implored Jean Rio to accompany him to California she leaped at the opportunity. She had not seen her sons John and Charles in more than a decade, and correspondence with them had been sporadic at best, especially in the highly charged atmosphere during the years leading up to and following the Utah War. Her midwife's notebooks filled with jottings from this period—distinctly different from the long prose passages of her past—reflect a complacency and resignation notably different from the spirit of her earlier years, when she looked forward hopefully, never dwelling on the agony of the past or the fear of the unknown, but rather focusing on an excited and optimistic vision of the future. That was a time when frontier America appealed to her intellect and senses—before the promises were betrayed, the hopes deferred. Now, on November 22, 1869, she is fully in the moment, open to change while devoid of expectation. "I shall see my two boys again and hope to enjoy the time," she writes in the first entry she has made in her emigration diary in seventeen years. "How long I shall remain is uncertain, but I have learned to lean on my heavenly father for direction so I do not feel much concerned for the future."

CHAPTER NINE

One Household of Faith

T HE TRAIN LUMBERED over the snowdrifts of the Sierras, a breathtaking view of Lake Tahoe in the distance. A new adventure had begun. California symbolized a rebirth for Jean Rio no less than England had meant a new life for her mother nearly a century earlier. How candid she was with Chauncey West about her decision to leave the church is unclear, though she brought all of her belongings with her. What is clear is that she shed her eighteen-year Mormon interlude as freely and completely as the surname Baker she had carried for thirty-two years, now calling herself Jean Rio Pearce.

Arriving in San Francisco with West on November 24, 1869, she waited at the railroad station for her son John, whom she had telegraphed to meet them. When he failed to appear she took her invalid companion to the sophisticated Cosmopolitan Hotel. Whatever she thought of this new and bustling city, when she saw her sons Charles, now thirty, and John, twenty-six, she knew it had to provide more opportunity and allure than the Deseret of their youth.

"My dear boy came to the hotel this morning," she wrote of

John. "What a change from the boy of seventeen when he took leave of me in Ogden ten years ago." A newlywed, John eagerly introduced his mother to Katie, "a whole-souled young woman," as Jean Rio described her, who was expecting their first child. Charles lived in an ornate Victorian home in the high style of the times—"he is very comfortably fixed"— which, after the poverty they had endured in Utah, was all the more impressive.

Jean Rio leased a "suite of rooms on Powell Street" for the rapidly declining Chauncey West, whose San Francisco doctor pronounced his infirmity "too deeply seated" to respond to treatment. On January 3, 1870, Jean Rio wrote that West was "unable to rise this morning." A week later he was dead. "The end has come," she wrote. "There has been a gradual sinking of the physical powers . . . at six this morning he expired. One of his hands was clasped in John's, the other in mine." Considering West's intimacy with Brigham Young and his own long-standing position in the Mormon hierarchy, that he wanted only Jean Rio, a disaffected Saint, and her apostate son John at his side at his time of death seems ironical at the least.

She accompanied West's body to Oakland, where family members retrieved it for the journey back to Utah for burial, and then she collapsed with fatigue. "I am weak in body, for my task has been a harassing one," she wrote. "For the last week I have never undressed, and the only rest I have taken has been lying down occasionally on the sofa." She continued on for a time at the Cosmopolitan before settling in with John and his wife in San Francisco while awaiting the birth of their child. Four months later she and the couple relocated to Sher-

man Island, a booming settlement in the delta at the conflu-
ence of the Sacramento and the San Joaquin rivers, approximately fifty miles northwest of San Francisco.

Entrepreneurs and farmers, recognizing the value of the
fertile swamplands, had poured into the area following the discovery of gold nearby in 1848. Reclamation and settlement of
the delta was peaking as the completion of the transcontinental
railroad freed more than twelve thousand Chinese migrant
workers, most of whom moved into the delta to work on the
levees that were under construction, on vast farms that produced asparagus and rice, and in canneries and nearby coal
mines. The huge, once-useless marshland was being transformed into what would become a historic labyrinth of inter-
connected waterways and rich reclaimed islands. When the
1868 California legislature removed acreage ownership limita-
tions, John Baker seized the opportunity and claimed for himself a large tract of land. By April 1870, six months after her
arrival in California, Jean Rio had moved into a comfortable
home that John had built on Sherman Island for his wife, baby
son, and mother. "It is like being in a new world," she writes in
a brief entry at the end of her emigration diary.

Always an avid observer of nature, she was overwhelmed
by the lushness of the land, which was filled with migratory
waterfowl, hundreds of species of fish, much other wildlife,
and wild herbs and other plants. Jean Rio never failed to recognize beauty, whether in the storm of the sea, the heat of the
plains, or the poverty of her farm. But after the desolation and
adversity of Deseret, the copiousness of the delta must have
seemed an especially blessed reward. She sent word to her son

Walter that opportunity was abundant, and within months he, along with his wife, Eliza, and their eight children, arrived from Utah as well. Jean Rio's sister-in-law and her husband, Mary Ann and Jeremiah Bateman, who had accompanied her twenty years earlier from England to Utah, soon followed. The last to arrive was her daughter, Elizabeth, whose husband, Lewis West, died of smallpox during the summer of 1870, leaving her a widow with five small children. Polygamist son William would be the only Baker to stay behind in Utah, the only member of the family to remain a practicing Mormon.

Jean Rio brought with her on the train to California all that remained of the possessions she had taken across the Atlantic Ocean and Great Plains, a collection of belongings much reduced from her sojourn in Zion. Her posterity, her legacy, her passion, and her accomplishment were inextricably tied to her square grand piano, but that was now in Brigham Young's possession. The only vestige she brought of it to her new home was the black, tar-coated crate that had kept it safe through all its crossings, a container that she valued enough to save. (The crate is said to be in a California museum.) She had always loved beautiful clothing. She had needed an extensive wardrobe of fine dresses for her singing performances, and had taken those and more to be worn in Zion. Those dresses that were left were threadbare, the others had long since been cut up and remade into clothing more suitable for frontier life. She had her sapphire ring and her gold band, a writing desk and printed music, a black shawl she had brought from England, and the only piece of bone china left from the set of dishes that had been her mother's. Every Christmas since her arrival in

America she had served plum pudding on this "blue willow ware platter," surrounding the dessert with holly and topping it with brandy, which was set aflame.

In 1871 the "big flood," as it was referred to locally, wiped out the Sherman Island settlement, and the Baker clan moved to the small town of Antioch nearby. Founded in 1849 by a man named Joseph Smith, which the Baker family found ironic, the community was a boomtown reaping the economic benefits of the delta reclamation. Keeping a hand in farming, the Baker men branched out into politics and other community enterprises, becoming merchants as well. The name Rio became ubiquitous in the area—all eight of Walter's offspring had it as a middle name—and was now pronounced with the soft *i* as if derived from the Spanish word for "river," the name being mistakenly associated with early Mexican influence in the territory.

Son Charles remained in San Francisco, where he and his wife had ten children; he apparently practiced law and made a fortune that surpassed any of his brothers'. John continued rice farming while pursuing local politics; eventually he became a Republican state legislator. He became known for introducing antipolygamy legislation, but since he kept his Mormon past private, his constituents would not have been aware of the rich origins of that legislation. He built a mansion at Emmaton on Sherman Island for his family, which ultimately would include four children. Increasingly, he spent much of his time in Sacramento, the state capital, forty miles away, traveling upriver by paddleboat.

Walter built a home in Antioch, and Jean Rio divided her

time between the two nearby sons' residences, traveling between the locations by ferry. Her growing Baker grandsons were volunteers for the local fire department, members of the Masonic lodge (this was widely considered a public rejection and disavowal of Mormonism), and owners of a hardware store and a pharmacy. Josiah Elliott Rio Baker, believed by other descendants to have been Jean Rio's favorite grandson as the namesake of the beloved child she had buried at sea, became postmaster and Contra Costa County treasurer. Wearing a cutaway coat and stylish straw hat, Josiah was a well-known figure in town, his hardware store offering utilitarian supplies as well as the latest fashions. "In addition to the merchandise you'd expect, such as nails, farm implements, tools, etc.," an Antioch newspaper noted, "the store also sold furniture, carpets, wallpaper, stove oil . . . [and] a sign over the main entrance advertised Eureka Stoves and Ranges, which were among the first mass-produced kitchen appliances."

Determined not to be a burden to her family, Jean Rio had immediately thrown herself into a newfound social, political, and professional life. "I mean to work at my trade," she writes in 1870 in a passage entered in her emigration diary. But while her "trade" had been dressmaking in Ogden, it would be midwifery in California. She became active with the local temperance chapter, part of a wide-ranging and long-misunderstood social reform movement advocating not only the prohibition of alcohol because of its destructive impact on families and society but also woman suffrage, equal pay, birth control, child labor reform, and the eight-hour day. She was responsible for Antioch's first high school, and she was an unrelenting advocate for such community services and facilities as a library, a fire truck, and a public park. She joined Eastern Star, the women's equivalent of the Masonic lodge, and became a faithful and devoted member of the First Congregational Church of Antioch. The first church of any kind in the community, it had been formed a few years earlier and was known for its socially conscious and politically liberal attitudes. It proudly accepted an African-American member—it was the first church in California to do so—and served as a school for children of the local Chinese laborers; such demonstrations of tolerance were otherwise unheard of at the time. Jean Rio never spoke of her years in Utah, and apparently neither she nor her sons ever told the California offspring of their Mormon experience. Whether fearful of reprisals or simply desirous of putting that past firmly behind them, once in California the Baker family truly began anew.

Jean Rio's life was a steady stream of delivering babies, sewing dresses for her young granddaughters, making hats for her two daughters-in-law, attending temperance meetings and church services, and nursing those in the community who were sick. She kept an extensive midwife's notebook, itemizing the daily events that occupied her time, the childbirth dramas and rousing sermons, the Bible readings and deathbed vigils. She made "pettycoats and underclothes" for "Aunt Bateman," and calico and gingham costumes for her granddaughters' dolls.

It's unclear what became of the substantial "lifetime annuity" she had inherited from her aristocratic great-uncle William Rio MacDonald, but she lived as a woman of means during her Antioch years, on a scale that obviously exceeded her earnings as a midwife. It was a dramatic contrast to the utter poverty she had suffered in Utah after turning over all of her property and money to the church. Perhaps her deceased husband Edward Pearce had left her an estate, or perhaps once out of Utah she was able to reestablish contact with English relatives or lawyers who might have facilitated a release of her inheritance, bypassing its arrogation by Brigham Young. In the event, at a time when the annual median income in Antioch was approximately $500, she had the wherewithal to lend the Masons $1,000—the equivalent of more than $17,000 in 2004 currency—for which she received as collateral a mortgage on the Masonic temple. She also purchased an expensive, prestigious handcrafted Mason & Hamlin reed organ—her first musical instrument since relinquishing her Collard & Collard piano to Young—and had it shipped by rail from Boston to Antioch.

"My life bids fair to be a very quiet one," she wrote. "I have every temporal comfort my heart can desire, my children vie with each other in contributing to my happiness." Still, by 1875 a restless desire to see her son William and his children (some of whom she had never met) overtook her, and she began making plans for an extended visit back to Utah Territory. Meanwhile, her widowed daughter Elizabeth had remarried and was living again in Ogden—now practicing Mormonism after a period of lapsed faith—and Jean Rio was eager to see her and meet her recently born grandchildren as well.

"In August 1875," she wrote later, "I returned to Utah to

visit my remaining children, and many friends whom I love and esteem, as the members of one household of Faith, irrespective of creed."

That summer of 1875, Utah Territory was agitated with the upcoming trial of John Doyle Lee, the man now called "the butcher in chief" by the *Salt Lake Daily Tribune,* accused for his role in the Mountain Meadows Massacre. National newspapers were covering the sensational story of the mass murder that had occurred eighteen years earlier. In the intervening years, the massacre had been the focus of passionate debate, both within Utah Territory and in the nation at large. At issue were the alleged acquiescence, culpability, and cover-up by Brigham Young. In the immediate aftermath of the massacre, the church began placing the blame on Lee, an adopted son of Young, portraying him as a fanatical zealot who had acted without authority from Young or the church hierarchy. Now, maneuvering for statehood and facing mounting pressure from the U.S. government, along with a national outcry for justice in the matter, Young's theocracy was forced to hold someone accountable for the crimes.

Though at the time of the massacre Jean Rio had been living in Ogden—three hundred miles north of the site—her sons who had been required to serve in the church's militia would have been privy to reports and rumors of the event that swirled through Utah, especially among men in the military ranks. As noted earlier, two of her sons, Charles and John, had abandoned both Utah and the Mormon Church in 1858—the year following the massacre—in direct response to the terrible incident, according to their descendants. Now, on her return to Utah, Jean Rio found herself situated less than sixty miles from where the "trial of the century"—what a Salt Lake City newspaper was calling "the most important criminal case ever tried in the United States"—had begun two weeks earlier. In a different time and place Jean Rio might have been an alert chronicler of such events, though at this point her diary is enigmatically silent on the subject, suggesting that the long arm of retribution was still intimidating to apostates.

If Jean Rio and her last remaining Mormon son now disagreed about Mormon theology, church corruption, and the doctrine of polygamy, they apparently put such discord aside during her visit to his Richfield home. Ensconced at the gracious residence of William's first wife, Hannah, Jean Rio determined to enjoy her son and his family for what she clearly believed would be the last time.

At the direction of Brigham Young, William had settled the picturesque little farming community of Richfield in Sevier County in 1863. By 1867 the Indian uprising that would become known as Utah's Black Hawk War intensified, and the town was abandoned. William had relocated his wives, Hannah and Nicolena, and their numerous children to the community of Nephi, seventy-five miles north. They had remained there until 1872, when the fighting subsided and he could safely return his families to the two homes he had built for them in Richfield—Hannah's large adobe and Nicolena's dugout.

At the moment of Jean Rio's last visit to Utah, the place seemed suddenly to occupy the front pages of newspapers around the country. While John Doyle Lee's trial brought hundreds of journalists and federal officials into the territory, now too was polygamy bringing renewed and unwanted outside attention to the controversial theocratic enclave. Fanny Stenhouse, the Englishwoman and former Saint, had begun a nationwide lecture series promoting her new book-length exposé on the Mormon Church and polygamy, *Tell It All.* Harriet Beecher Stowe had written the preface to Stenhouse's book, and the subject was arousing men and women throughout the country to demand that polygamy be eradicated.

It would be but a few more years until William George Baker would be forced into hiding for his principles, seeking to escape the wrath of the U.S. marshals enforcing antipolygamy statutes. (Such enforcement was a condition for Utah statehood.) For now, he believed in the doctrine as the divine inspiration of Mormon prophets, and he practiced plural marriage openly, proudly, and enthusiastically. Considered an upright and noble man, courteous and kind—if perhaps a bit stern and dour for Jean Rio's taste—William was one of the leaders of the community. "Make yourself an honest man, and then you may be sure there is one rascal less in the world" was his motto. A man who "never bamboozled or bribed," as one account described him, he was a lawyer, hotelier, city councilman, justice of the peace, notary public, county assessor, and dramatist, and he held the coveted U.S. Postal Service contracts to deliver mail by Pony Express. Having inherited his father's engineering aptitude, he devised a reservoir for melting snow and an ingenious irrigation system.

"Medium tall, with steel blue eyes, gray and black wavy

William George Baker, Jean Rio's second oldest son,
remained a staunchly loyal Mormon despite the apostasy
of his mother and brothers.

hair, and a curly beard, which was always well trimmed," as one of his daughters described him, "he stood very erect and had a portly bearing." The daughter remembered his voice especially: "He had a deep baritone." He was known for always riding a prancing black stallion, and in the Fourth of July and Pioneer Day parades he proudly donned the military uniform of Brigham Young's controversial Nauvoo Legion, "epaulettes, sword, and all," according to one account.

Jean Rio marveled at her forty-year-old son's unwavering faith, the awesome financial burden of providing for two wives and the first fifteen of what would be twenty-three children, and the adversity he was willing to endure in pursuit of the everlasting. "Plucked from the lap of luxury and set down in a frontier land of staggering toil and comfortless surroundings," recalled one of his children, not totally objectively, "he tackled his job and made good without excuses or regrets. His brothers couldn't stand the privations and hardships and moved to California where life was not so hard. But William stayed with the religion he had embraced as a boy." Soft-spoken, he had a gentility that commanded attention. Every Sunday morning, a granddaughter recalled, Jean Rio watched as he shined all the children's shoes at both homes, placing them in a row, smallest to largest, "in a precise line like little black soldiers."

"I remained among them one year and nine months, and had the chance of traveling over more of the Territory than I did during my eighteen years of residence there," Jean Rio recalled in her diary. She helped William organize the first dramatic company in Richfield, producing their first play in an old meeting house. She sewed strips of unbleached muslin together for a stage curtain. Using lampblack, soot, and other vegetable dyes that she mixed with oil, she painted a scenic landscape of flowers and shrubs, and she hung the curtain from a stout cottonwood pole. She then acted in the first play produced there, *The Lady of Lyons,* in which William starred in the role of Claude Melnotte. A perennial favorite of Victorian theater, the Edward Lytton play, set in post-Revolution France, was a sophisticated romantic comedy about the pretensions of class.

Still, for all the lightheartedness and laughter, Jean Rio, almost sixty-seven, returned to Antioch with mixed feelings: "In April 1877 I came back to California, and though I left Utah with regret, feeling sure that I should never see my dear ones there again on Earth, still, with much thankfulness that all was well with them," she wrote later.

Three years after her visit to Utah, on May 8, 1880, she penned her final entry in the surviving diary.

I am seventy years old this day. Well may I say, "hitherto hath the Lord helped me." I have good health and am spending my time among my children, sometimes at one house, sometimes at another. My boys have met with many disappointments, many trials, not the least has been the death of Chauncy, Walter's youngest son. The rest of the family are well, and still are working on, hoping for better times. I can truly say, I have but one wish unfulfilled, and that is that I may live to see every one of my children and grandchildren faithful members of the Kingdom of God. I cannot expect to see many more birthdays, and as every hour brings me nearer to the final one, I feel to say with Toplady [the famous eighteenth-century British clergyman and hymnist]:

> *When I draw this fleeting breath,*
> *When my eyelids close in death*
> *When I soar to worlds unknown*
> *And behold the judgment throne,*
> *Rock of Ages, shelter me,*
> *Let me hide myself in Thee.*

Peace at Last

JULY 25, 1883

From Henry Walter Baker, Los Medanos, California
To William George Baker, Richfield, Utah

I am sorry to be obliged to write you this time in a not very
happy frame of mind. Yesterday was my 50th birthday and I
had the melancholy task to perform, of burying Dear
Mother. She died quite suddenly on the night of the 21st at
Los Gatos. I received a telegram Sunday noon and started
immediately, to bring home her remains. Yesterday I placed
her in the [Oddfellows] burying ground, near Antioch, and
alongside of my Chauncy.

This trouble, although looked for for a good while,
seemed to be a surprise after all. She had a malignant cancer
and suffered a very great deal, and prayed for her release
many a time, and it is a great blessing to her, I am sure, to be
saved from lingering any longer. She was a member of the
Antioch Congregational Church, and we had the funeral
there.

... The people of Los Gatos were very kind indeed; I never saw a better feeling manifested anywhere. All seemed determined to do any and everything for the comfort of the family in their affliction.

> *Your affectionate brother,*
> *H. W. Baker*

Formal and aloof, this letter epitomizes the breach between the California branch of the Baker family and the one son— my great-grandfather—remaining in Utah. The letter, like Jean Rio's last will and testament, does not begin to explain the life of this remarkable woman. Among the mysteries is how she happened to die in Los Gatos, a small village at the base of the Santa Cruz Mountains seventy-five miles south of Antioch. She had apparently moved there with her son John and his family. Famous for its sanitariums, the town had become a center for patients suffering from respiratory problems, including tuberculosis, but there is no evidence that she or any of her family members had such an affliction. In 1881, thirty-eight-year-old John had become very ill and had taken to performing his legislative business from a hotel bed in Sacramento. He died quite suddenly that year. He is buried in the state plot at the California capitol.

On June 6, 1882, Jean Rio drafted her final will.

I, Jean Rio Pearce (née Baker), widow, being of sound mind and in physical health, do make this my last will and testament. I have lived (and hope to die) in firm belief and faith in

Jesus Christ, as the son of God, the only atonement for sin, and the only way of salvation. It is my express desire that my body be placed for burial, in a <u>quite plain redwood coffin</u>, without any manner of ornamentation, and that I be buried as near as possible to my grandson, Chauncy Rio Baker. And that my elder sons, and grandsons, act as attendants at my funeral, and themselves lower my Body into the grave.

Naming her oldest son, Henry Walter Baker, her executor, she dispersed property equally among her four surviving children, Walter, William, Charles, and Elizabeth, with John's share going to his two young daughters. It was an estate worth approximately $35,000 by today's standards.

In the end, for all the thousands of words she wrote, much of her life remains shrouded. I reassembled her story from untold shattered pieces. In doing so I met and corresponded with dozens of her descendants—the grandchildren and great-grandchildren of Walter, William, Charles, Elizabeth, and John—many of whom had had tiny shards of oral history handed down to them. Except for the Utah descendants of William, these "cousins" were uniformly unaware of the Baker family's Mormon experience, so anonymously assimilated in secular California life had Jean Rio and her sons and their descendants become.

The California Bakers remained in the Antioch and San Francisco vicinities for the following generations. As for William's descendants, most of the children from his first family remained faithful members of the Mormon Church, while many of those born to my great-grandmother Nicolena, includ-

Mormon apostle Wilford Woodruff, who as a young missionary had baptized William George Baker in London in 1849. His proclamation abolishing polygamy forty-one years later would make criminal fugitives of William George Baker and other men who devoutly practiced polygamy.

ing my grandmother Hazel, left the faith. Following church president Wilford Woodruff's proclamation abolishing the Mormon practice of polygamy in 1890—which meant that only the first wife could be legally recognized—Nicolena was left to fend for herself and her large family in a primitive village in south-central Utah. Ironically, Woodruff had been the missionary who had converted and then baptized William Baker as a young man in London. In one of those strange twists of fate, Woodruff issued the edict that would send William Baker into hiding and ultimately result in his incarceration as a polygamist. Ordered to divide his property and cash among his two families, and required to provide for them financially, he found the task impossible. Despite his ample income, there was simply not enough to support two wives and eighteen children—two of Hannah's and three of Nicolena's had died.

Nicolena suddenly found herself a forty-five-year-old mother of seven with little if any outside support. She, like hundreds of other polygamist women in her position, received no financial aid from the church, of which she had been a devout member for some thirty-five years since her epic walk across the country to Zion. Nor was the husband upon whom she was depending to pull her "through the veil" to everlasting deliverance able to provide much assistance. He wrote to her while a fugitive from the U.S. marshals.

Dear Lena,

Tell Bro. Warrock I will send the rent to him in a few days. Do not be uncaring about me, as I shall return soon . . . it is not wisdom for me to come home. If you knew how disappointed I feel I know you would favor me with a letter, tell me all of the news, especially what is being done by [the] court.

Give my love and kisses to the children and be assured I am still lovingly yours—

W.G.B.

> You must enclose your letter to me <u>sealed</u> inside of
> another envelope addressed to "Sam E. Jost," Ogden City,
> Utah.

Still, the adversity seems to have strengthened her own faith, as she continued tithing her diminutive income while she disappointedly watched her children fall away from the church. In the 1890s she boldly ventured into a millinery business, earning enough to support her children and even provide them with an education. When William died in 1901 he received a substantial obituary reflective of his long-standing stature in the community of Richfield. Neither Nicolena nor any of his children by her was named as next of kin. Like the thousands of other children of polygamists, they were treated as if they were illegitimate and in effect punished by disinheritance and social stigma by the very society that had sanctioned and encouraged the practice of polygamy.

So what do we know of Jean Rio Griffiths Baker Pearce? We are sure of her deepest faith. We are sure of how much she loved her family and of how much they loved her. We are sure of what she expected of the new Zion in America, and therefore we know how deep her disillusionment with that society and culture was, how repelled she was by the suppression of women, by the avarice of this "Kingdom of God upon Earth," by the atrocity of Mountain Meadows. She took her family and most of her material possessions, including her beloved piano, and crossed half a world in search of a community of faith that would bring into practical existence the principles of the New Testament that she believed in—compassion, tolerance, love, reconciliation. What she found instead was a patriarchal theocracy fiercely committed to prejudice and material greed, turning upon its own members the weapons of fear and intimidation that had been used against the faith in its infancy. But we can be sure that as her disillusionment grew she faced it the same way she had faced her other trials—the deaths of her husbands and children, the storms at sea. We have the testimony of her granddaughter: Jean Rio met "the most terrifying situations with a calmness of spirit. She had compassion for the downtrodden, sympathy for the underprivileged."

In my view, what Jean Rio came to at the end of this century of tumult, of promise and betrayal, was a very modern theology—a tolerance that led her to hope for a community of faith irrespective of creed. The twenty-first century is undergoing throughout the world a clash of creeds more ferocious and dangerous than anything in Jean Rio's world. We have never been more in need of the tolerance, respect, and freedom from religious dogmatism that she embodied, the principles she hoped to leave to posterity. In search of fundamental Christianity, she came to the conclusion that fundamentalism was narrow and barren. In search of a kind of organizing creed, she understood that creed often confines rather than enables true faith. Crossing a world to find a material or geographical place of enlightenment, she, like many seekers, found that her spiritual home had always been within herself.

She was one of the more notable apostates of the Mormon Church, yet the church never acknowledges her apostasy. She was one of the most disillusioned converts to the faith, and yet she is used as a recruitment and proselytizing tool in the temple's video display. She represents one of the religion's more notable failures, and yet she is advertised as one of its successes.

For so many years, Jean Rio was deprived her voice. Then the church distorted it. My goal has been to restore it.

NOTES

Beyond Jean Rio's emigration diary and midwife's notebook, as well as family papers accumulated over the years, my portrait of her and her children, of their remarkable journey and its sequels, and of the era in which they all lived draws on a number of primary and secondary sources in the history of the American West. The bibliography that follows these notes supplements and expands on the diary and personal papers as indicated below. All conditions of life and landscape, as well as states of mind and the context of historical events, have documentary support.

PREFACE:
AN EXTRAORDINARY WOMAN OF ORDINARY VIRTUES

xvii "Women have not been well served": Moynihan, Armitage, and Dichamp, xi.

xvii "Pioneering is really a wilderness experience": Immigrant Lulu Fuhr, in Stratton, 33.

CHAPTER ONE: "WORTH A LONG WALK TO SEE"

3 The episode re-created here is detailed in the Jean Rio midwife's notebook from 1873.

CHAPTER TWO: A WINE CASK ON THE CHANNEL

5 "an instrument adopted": Harrison and Sullivan, 649.

5 "Hourly, the hideous instrument of torture:" Baroness Emmu-

ska Orczy, *The Scarlet Pimpernel* (1902; New York: Signet, 2002), 2.

5 "The mechanism falls": J.-I. Guillotin, quoted in Brazen Kallisti, "The Chapel Perilous," historical Web site, www.sepulchritude.com/.

7 "Men in women's clothes": Orczy, *The Scarlet Pimpernel*, 2.

8 "The English never ceased to wonder": Weiner, 45.

8 THE BACKGROUND OF SUSANNA BURGESS: The surviving records of the marriage of Susanna and John only add to the larger mystery around Susanna's family origins and her dramatic deliverance from revolutionary France. The first any of Jean Rio's descendants from the twentieth century learned of her mother's escape from France was in a letter from Jean Rio's granddaughter Katie Baker to another granddaughter, Hazel Baker Denton, in 1951. (Katie Elizabeth Rio Baker was the last-born child of Jean Rio's son Henry Walter Baker. She was born in Utah in 1868.) Hazel wrote the following regarding the episode:

> A certain family in Paris at that time [1789], whose name we have never been able to trace, concerns all of us. It was the family of Jean Rio's mother, who at that horrible time was the family's baby girl.
>
> We know from the story that the family did not belong to the French royalty, but to the well-to-do, well-educated, and high-minded middle classes, who, along with the Royalists, became victims of the hatred of the Revolutionists. All members of this French family (who are our ancestors) were guillotined—all, that is, except their infant daughter. She was saved by one of their faithful manservants. He somehow managed, by concealing the tiny girl in a wine casque, to smuggle her across the English Channel into England. In England he became her guardian; very likely gave her a different,

and almost certainly an English, name, for French refugees at the time had a price on their heads and were hunted down by French officials for a great many years, until Napoleon came into power as Emperor of France and welcomed all French refugees to return. However, our little French girl grew up in England, and very naturally she and her benefactor became accustomed to, and took on, English ways. We can imagine the faithful servant was very fond of his fledgling and gave her every possible care, though we have no idea how long he lived to care for her, nor at what age she moved into Scotland or why. It could well be that during their lives together he made it his duty to tell her all about her family's fate—enough of it to instill into her young mind a hatred for the French. When she moved into Scotland she married a Scot, whose name was Griffiths. In due time a girl baby was born to them. They named her Jean Rio, and it was the Scotch Jean, not the French spelling Jeanne. When this Jean Rio, who became our grandmother, grew up, it can be presumed that her mother told her the family story, by which means the hatred for the French was so deeply impressed upon her that it stayed with her even up to the time when, in San Francisco, she told the story to her granddaughter Katie Baker, who, many years later [1951], wrote the details of the tragedy to me.

A Salt Lake City, Utah, genealogical research firm reported to members of the Baker family in 2002 that it was unable to trace the roots of Susanna Burgess.

THE RIO FAMILY OF CHARD, ENGLAND: A review of government indices in Chard revealed one reference to a Thomas Henry MacDonald Rio in a "volume of minutes (1870–1940), which contains a resolution from the charitable bequest of

T.H.M. Rio, 1868, and copies of Rio's Charity Scheme and associated documents, 1889–1909." According to an archivist with the Somerset (England) Archives, "The bequest for a charity suggests that the Rio family may have been quite a rich and prominent family in the area." Hazel's own father, William George Baker (Jean Rio's son), told Hazel that he had "French blood mixed up with his English" that came from Jean Rio's ancestry. According to Etta Jacks, granddaughter of Henry Walter and Eliza Ann Elliott Baker, "Daddy used to tell that [Jean Rio] was a member of the MacDonald clan, that her people 'away back when' used to be the 'Lairds of the Isle of Skye,' but they rebelled against the King and their lands were confiscated." Author's collection of papers.

9 "With a price of thirty thousand pounds": Herman, 158.

9 RIO FAMILY GENEALOGY: AncestryPlus.com, Family Search. com, and various other genealogy Web sites contain information on the Rio and Rioux (sometimes spelled "Riou" and "Rieux" as well) families. The largest emigration of Rioux family members from France seems to have occurred in the eighteenth century, when many members of the clan resettled in Quebec, Canada.

10 "The worst excesses": Hibbert, 227.

12 "As a rule, when girls had left school": Crosland, 66.

12 "reading and writing": Herman, 24.

12 "the least thought-inspiring": Crosland, 66.

12 "no waste of time": Ibid.

13 proximity to the royal family: Hazel Baker Denton recalled sitting "wide-eyed for hours" as her father, William George Baker, described "how beautiful Queen Victoria was; about her crown, her jewels, her fabulous silk and velvet dresses, and her Parliament robes trimmed with ermine," which he had seen many times.

13 "They were taught personal cleanliness": Hazel Baker Denton, author's collection.

14 Jean Rio's paternal great-uncle: His last will and testament, extant in "The Probate Record for William Rio McDonald, Doctor of Physic," is a fascinating and vitally revealing document. Regarding the Scottish ancestry of the family he makes the following reference:

> To my niece Jane Baker (daughter of my nephew Walter Griffiths) & to her husband, Henry Baker, each of them five guineas for mourning at the death of my wife. I bequeath to my nephew Walter Griffiths my gold watch & seals excepting my seal with my arms engraven in it which (after my wife's death) I bequeath to my respected cousin Robert Rio of Chard, Somerset, and also my coat of arms in a gilt frame with two small prints in the frame of THE HOUSE CALLED ARMIDALE at SLATE in THE ISLE OF SKYE SCOTLAND.

15 "Its politics were stuck": Herman, 267–268.
16 "When the inner cities are crying": Chadwick, 75.
16 "Its piety tended to be sober" . . . "Romantic literature and art": Chadwick, 17.
17 "felt as close to Abraham": Moorman, 373.
20 "The theory that the Americans are of Jewish origin": Hubert Howe Bancroft, quoted in Brodie, 45. Brodie writes of the widely held opinion of the time that the American Indians were descendants of the lost tribe:

> Fantastic parallels were drawn between Hebraic and Indian customs, such as feasts of first fruits, sacrifices of the firstborn in the flock, cities of refuge, ceremonies of purification, and division into tribes. The Indian "language" (which actually consisted of countless distinct languages derived from numerous linguistic stocks) was said to be chiefly Hebrew. The Indian belief in the Great

Spirit (which originally had been implanted by French and Spanish missionaries) was said to be derived in a direct line from Jewish monotheism. One writer even held that syphilis, the Indian's gift to Europe, was an altered form of Biblical leprosy. (Brodie, 45)

21 "In no other period in American history": Brodie, 101.

21 "The literalist Mormon timetable": Coates, 89.

22 "Mormonism is an eclectic religious philosophy": John Gunnison, quoted in Fielding, 8.

22 "Joseph had convincing answers": Krakauer, 112.

24 "There is a strange power": Fanny Stenhouse, 41.

CHAPTER THREE: THESE LATTER DAYS

26 "Mormons must be treated as enemies": Lillburn W. Boggs, quoted in Brodie, 235.

27 "Young arose and roared": Lee, *Writings*, 142.

28 "Every sentiment and feeling": Brigham Young sermon, June 12, 1860, *Journal of Discourses* 8:294.

29 "a police state in Nauvoo": Hirshson, quoted in Coates, 54.

30 "The prophet, through the sheer force of his personality": Coates, 55.

30 "In the New World": Reisner, 4.

32 "sin and unworthiness": Taylor, 19.

33 "preaching the glory of America": Brodie in Piercy, xiv.

34 "the working-class Mormon response": Jensen and Thorp, xiii.

35 "It was deeply subversive": Hazleton, 50.

35 "One must be called": Heilbrun, 23.

36 "according to the orders": Emigrant Hannah Tapfield King, quoted in Bartholomew, 71.

38 the crate . . . was dipped in tar: The "black box," as the piano crate was known, is reportedly housed in a museum in California, though the exact location is unknown to the author.

39 "a formidable gauntlet of wind and wave": Sonne, *Saints on the Seas,* 53.

CHAPTER FOUR: COMMITTED TO THE DEEP

43 "schooners, barks, barkentines": Sonne, *Saints on the Seas,* 34.
43 "a typical product of Yankee shipwrights": Sonne, *Ships, Saints, and Mariners,* 87.
44 "The funds are appropriated in the form of a loan": Brigham Young, October 16, 1849, quoted in Piercy, xvii.
46 "the perfect order and propriety": Dickens, 449.
49 "Now it shall come to pass": Isaiah, 2:2, *Holy Bible, New King James Version, Reader's Edition.*
55 There had been one marriage, three births, and two conversions of crew members, and the only tragedy to mark the voyage was the death of Josiah Baker who had been suffering from consumption when he boarded the ship.
55 "ardent spirits": Piercy, 71.

CHAPTER FIVE: SNAGS AND SAWYERS

65 "floating palaces": Piercy, 73.
75 "The teamster should drive": Ibid., 106.

CHAPTER SIX: THE CROSSING

88 "flee Babylon": Black and Porter, ix.
88 "Buffalo, elk, deer": Lee, *Journals,* 117.
89 "In the cove of mountains": Frémont's report, quoted in Wise, 78.
89 "the bloodthirsty Christians": Bagley, 19.
89 "Word and Will of the Lord": De Voto, 452.
90 "Zion shall be established": Lee, quoted in Brooks, 139.
91 "9 rods wide and 3 feet deep": Piercy, 108.
92 "A nothing river": Michener, 23.

94 "Our Encampment": *Trail of Hope: The Story of the Mormon Trail.* PBS, September 26, 1997.

95 "No person who has not": Ibid.

102 "The campsites were bad": Kimball and Kimball, 31.

CHAPTER SEVEN: A LIFE OF TOIL

113 "place where the land is acknowledged": Thomas Bullock, quoted in Bigler, 39.

113 "The communal food gatherers": Bigler, 39.

113 "He renders no account": T. B. H. Stenhouse, 665.

114 "Different methods were used": David Bigler, interview by author, July 28, 2003.

114 "Stone of Daniel": Bigler, 16.

114 "And in the days of these kings": Daniel 2:44, *Holy Bible, New King James Version, Reader's Edition.*

117 "instruments of torture": Hazel Baker Denton, *Ironing Days,* 59.

118 "Castle of Spiders": Walker and Dant, 121.

118 "This is a hideous place": Ibid.

118 "Sometimes as many as 60": Walker and Dant, 123.

120 "the pinnacle of post-mortal existence": Coates, 81.

120 "Hence all true Mormons are Priests": Mary Ettie V. Smith, in Green, 154.

120 "the lowest rung": Coates, 77.

121 "They [the Mormons] are Jews": Burton, 397.

121 "Each wife would be chosen": Seagraves, 81.

122 "Out of this matter grows an immense power": Gunnison, 71.

124 "a life so unremittingly tough": Robert Coles, in Forward to Schlissel, Gibbens, and Hampsten, vii.

126 "the transformation of the home": Hardy, 40.

126 "the curse pronounced on Ham": Ibid., 39.

128 "This little family of Londoners": Hazel Baker Denton, 1951 Baker family reunion record.

128 "The Baker men": Author's collection of family papers.

131 "afford to purchase wagons": Brigham Young, from the *Millennial Star,* December 22, 1855, quoted in Hirshson, 152.

131 "thrown back upon my old plan": Ibid.

131 "With a morsel of bread": T.B.H. Stenhouse, 338–339. On the handcart disaster, see also Bigler, 104 ff.

132 "Backsliders were to be hewn down": Gibbs, 8 ff.

133 "There are sins that can be atoned for": Brigham Young, quoted in *Deseret News,* October 1, 1856.

136 "The whole United States rang with its horrors": Twain, 428.

136 "We intend to desolate the Territory": Brigham Young and his commander Daniel Wells to David Evans, September 16, 1857, reprinted in Bigler, 148.

137 "I am your leader": Brigham Young's instructions and remarks in March 1858, reprinted in Hirshson, 179.

138 "The brothers sneaked away": Barbara Baker, interview by author, December 27, 2002.

139 "a pageant of divine destiny": Udall, 108.

CHAPTER EIGHT: THROUGH THE VEIL

141 "The monotony of a man's life": Laxness, 17.

141 "The Danes, proverbially reluctant": Mulder, x.

143 "In Scandinavia": Ibid., 72.

144 "Keep clean": Nicolena Bertelsen's recollection as told to her daughter Hazel Baker Denton. Author's collection.

144 "digging in the sandy beaches": Ibid.

146 "She was, after all, a child": Ibid.

147 "Good taste in her own dress": Ibid.

149 "worst oppression and degradation": Fanny Stenhouse, ix.

150 "Even though Lena may not have been in love": "Portrait of a Danish Family," *Daughters of the Utah Pioneers,* Lessons for March and April, 1981, 303.

150 "She was the type of girl": Ibid., 302–03.

150 "bride's nest": Recollections of Nicolena's daughter Hazel Baker Denton, and 1951 Baker family reunion record.

151 "made her little home so clean": Recollection of Nicolena's daughter, Ruth Henrietta Baker Seegmiller, and 1951 Baker family reunion record.

151 "The little happinesses": Ibid.

154 "refugees from the Mormon kingdom": Aird, 197.

154 "Having through His Excellency": Ibid., 210.

154 "Next to winning the Civil War": Ambrose, 17

154 "thus ensuring an empire": Ibid., 18.

155 "never had taken the trouble": Fielding, 138.

155 "crossing the North Platte into the South Pass": Gunnison, 152.

156 "But the wording was vague" . . . "Just where this was to be": Quiett, in Wright and Swedenberg, 136.

157 "the Lord had revealed to him": Ibid., 137.

157 "cold and close": Brands, 425.

157 "called the faithful together": Quiett, in Wright and Swedenberg, 136.

157 "name his price": Ambrose, 282.

157 "The Lord, in another vision": Quiett, in Wright and Swedenberg, 137.

157 "to do the Union's grading": Brands, 425.

158 "calling on all the men": Ambrose, 283.

158 "received more than the contract price": "Utah, Our Pioneer Heritage" database though www.Ancestry.com.

159 "A great feat has been accomplished": *San Francisco Evening Bulletin,* April 29, 1869.

159 "As luck would have it": Brands, 436.

CHAPTER NINE: ONE HOUSEHOLD OF FAITH

166 THE CHILDREN OF JEAN RIO: Of nine children born to Jean Rio, two died in London, one died while crossing the Atlantic Ocean en route to America, and one died in Utah. By the time she relocated to Antioch, California, Jean Rio had five surviving children.

Henry Walter Baker was born July 24, 1833, in London. He married Eliza Ann Elliott in London on January 5, 1851, and accompanied his mother and siblings to America. Their children were Henry William Rio, Josiah Elliott Rio, Edward Bateman Rio, John Donald Rio, Alvin Walter Rio, Chauncy Alford Rio, Alice Jean Rio, and Katie Elizabeth Rio.

William George Baker was born June 10, 1835, in London. He married Hannah Hayward on November 25, 1855, and Nicolena Bertelsen on June 1, 1867. Children born to the first marriage were William George, Ruth Jean Rio, Henry, William Hayward, Frank Arnold, Mary Hannah Hayward, Walter, John Richard, Charles Fredrick, Elizabeth, Eugene Hayward, Claude Vincent, and Edward. Children born to the second marriage were Mary Ottomina, William Louis, Nelson, Lars Arthur, Annie Eliza, Ida Elizabeth, Ralph, Ruth Henrietta, Albert James, and Hazel Adelia.

Charles Edward Baker was born May 5, 1839, in London. He married Elizabeth Bird on November 20, 1858. Their children were Charles E., Walter, Annie C., Josephine Viola, Evangeline, Amy Jane, Frances Ethel, Sadie Maud, and Ernest.

Elizabeth Ann Baker was born May 20, 1841, in London. She married Lewis Alvin West on November 20, 1858. Following his death, she married Samuel Edward Jost on April 2, 1872. There were five children born to the first marriage: Lewis Alvin West, Adelia Eliza West, and three others who are unknown to the author. Children born to the second marriage were Mary Ann Frances

Jost, Katie Belle Jost, Lila E. Jost, Samuel Edward Jost, and Walter Jost.

John Edye Baker was born March 31, 1843, in London. He married Catherine Ann Franks in December 1868. Children born to this marriage were Melville, Jean Rio, Ida, and John Edye.

170 "the butcher in chief": *Salt Lake Daily Tribune,* November 14, 1874.
171 "the most important criminal case": *Salt Lake Daily Tribune,* July 19, 1875.
172 "Make yourself an honest man" . . . "He had a deep baritone": Descendants' recollections, author's collection.
173 "epaulettes, sword, and all" . . . "Plucked from the lap of luxury": Ibid.
174 "he tackled his job" . . . "in a precise line": Ibid.
175 "Toplady": Augustus Montague Toplady, the well-known eighteenth-century British clergyman and hymnist who wrote "Rock of Ages."

EPILOGUE: PEACE AT LAST

182 "the most terrifying situations": Descendants' recollections, author's collection.

BIBLIOGRAPHY

BOOKS

Ambrose, Stephen E. *Nothing Like It in the World: The Men Who Built the Transcontinental Railroad, 1863–1869.* New York: Simon & Schuster, 2000.

Armitage, Susan, et al., eds. *Women in the West: A Guide to Manuscript Sources.* New York: Garland, 1991.

Arrington, Leonard J. *Saints without Halos: The Human Side of Mormon History.* Salt Lake City: Signature Books, 1981.

Bagley, Will. *Blood of the Prophets: Brigham Young and the Massacre at Mountain Meadows.* Norman: University of Oklahoma Press, 2002.

Bain, David Haward. *Empire Express: Building the First Transcontinental Railroad.* New York: Viking, 1999.

Bartholomew, Rebecca. *Audacious Women: Early British Mormon Immigrants.* Salt Lake City: Signature Books, 1995.

Bible. *Holy Bible, New King James Version, Reader's Edition.* Nashville: Thomas Nelson, 1990.

Bigler, David L. *Forgotten Kingdom: The Mormon Theocracy in the American West, 1847–1896.* Logan: University of Utah Press, 1998.

Bitton, Davis. *Guide to Mormon Diaries and Autobiographies.* Provo, Utah: Brigham Young University Press, 1977.

Black, Susan Easton, and Larry C. Porter, eds. *Lion of the Lord: Essays on the Life and Service of Brigham Young.* Salt Lake City: Deseret Book Company, 1995.

Blessing, Marlene, ed. *A Road of Her Own: Women's Journeys in the West.* Golden, Colo.: Fulcrum, 2002.

Brands, H. W. *The Age of Gold: The California Gold Rush and the New American Dream.* New York: Doubleday, 2002.

Brodie, Fawn M. *No Man Knows My History: The Life of Joseph Smith, Mormon Prophet.* 2nd ed., rev. and enlarged. New York: Alfred A. Knopf, 1990.

Brooks, Juanita. *John Doyle Lee: Zealot, Pioneer Builder, Scapegoat.* 1962. Logan: Utah State University Press, 1992.

Burton, Richard Francis, Sir. *The City of the Saints, and across the Rocky Mountains to California.* New York: Harper & Brothers, 1862.

Carpenter, Kirsty. *Refugees of the French Revolution: Émigrés in London, 1789–1802.* New York: St. Martin's Press, 1999.

Chadwick, Owen. *The Spirit of the Oxford Movement: Tractarian Essays.* Cambridge: Cambridge University Press, 1990.

Cline, Cheryl. *Women's Diaries, Journals, and Letters: An Annotated Bibliography.* New York: Garland, 1989.

Coates, James. *In Mormon Circles: Gentiles, Jack Mormons, and Latter-day Saints.* Reading, Mass.: Addison-Wesley, 1991.

Crosland, Camilla Dufour Toulmin, "Mrs. Newton Crosland." *Landmarks of a Literary Life, 1820–1892.* London: Sampson Low, Marston & Company, 1893.

Denton, Hazel Baker. *Ironing Day.* New York: Exposition Press, 1955.

De Voto, Bernard. *The Year of Decision, 1846.* 1943. New York: Truman Talley Books / St. Martin's Press, 2000.

Donovan, Frank Robert. *River Boats of America.* New York: Thomas Y. Crowell, 1966.

Ellet, E. F. *Pioneer Women of the West.* New York: Charles Scribner, 1852.

Epstein, Barbara Leslie. *The Politics of Domesticity: Women, Evange-*

lism, and Temperance in Nineteenth-Century America. Middletown, Conn.: Wesleyan University Press, 1981.

Faulkner, George Washington. *Ho for California: The Faulkner Letters, 1875–1876.* Glendale, Calif.: 1964.

Fielding, R. Kent. *The Unsolicited Chronicler: An Account of the Gunnison Massacre, Its Causes and Consequences, Utah Territory, 1847–1859.* Brookline, Mass.: Paradigm Publications, 1993.

Gibbs, Josiah F. *The Mountain Meadows Massacre.* Salt Lake City: Salt Lake Tribune Publishing, 1910.

Green, Nelson Winch. *Fifteen Years Among the Mormons: Being a Narrative of Mrs. Mary Ettie V. Smith, Late of Great Salt Lake City.* New York: H. Dayton, 1859.

Greer, Donald. *The Incidence of the Emigration During the French Revolution.* Cambridge, Mass.: Harvard University Press, 1951.

Gunnison, J. W. *The Mormons, or Latter-Day Saints, In the Valley of The Great Salt Lake: A History of Their Rise and Progress, Peculiar Doctrines, Present Condition, and Prospects, Derived from Personal Observation, During a Residence Among Them.* Philadelphia: Lippincott, Grambo, 1852.

Hardy, B. Carmon. *Solemn Covenant: The Mormon Polygamous Passage.* Urbana: University of Illinois Press, 1992.

Harrison, John B., and Richard E. Sullivan. *A Short History of Western Civilization.* 3rd ed. New York: Alfred A. Knopf, 1971.

Hazleton, Lesley. *Mary: A Flesh-and-Blood Biography of the Virgin Mother.* London: Bloomsbury, 2004.

Heilbrun, Carolyn G. *Writing a Woman's Life.* New York: Ballantine Books, 1989.

Henrie, Samuel Nyal, ed. *Writings of John D. Lee.* Tucson, Ariz.: Hats Off Books, 2001.

Herman, Arthur. *How the Scots Invented the Modern World.* New York: Three Rivers Press / Crown, 2002.

Hibbert, Christopher. *Days of the French Revolution.* New York: Quill / Morrow, 1981.

Hirshson, Stanley P. *The Lion of the Lord: A Biography of Brigham Young.* New York: Alfred A. Knopf, 1969.

Jameson, Elizabeth, and Susan Armitage, eds. *Writing the Range: Race, Class, and Culture in the Women's West.* Norman: University of Oklahoma Press, 1997.

Jensen, Richard L., and Malcolm R. Thorp, eds. *Mormons in Early Victorian Britain.* Salt Lake City: University of Utah Press, 1989.

Kimball, Heber Chase. *On the Potter's Wheel: The Diaries of Heber C. Kimball.* Edited by Stanley B. Kimball. Salt Lake City: Signature Books, in assoc. with Smith Research Associates, 1987.

Kimball, Stanley B., and Violet T. Kimball. *Mormon Trail: Voyage of Discovery; The Story Behind the Scenery.* Las Vegas: KC Publications, 1995.

Kolodny, Annette. *The Land before Her: Fantasy and Experience of the American Frontiers, 1630–1860.* Chapel Hill: University of North Carolina Press, 1984.

Krakauer, Jon. *Under the Banner of Heaven: A Story of Violent Faith.* New York: Doubleday, 2003.

Laxness, Halldór. *Paradise Reclaimed.* New York: Vintage Books, 2002.

Lee, John D. *Journals of John D. Lee, 1846–1847 and 1859.* Edited by Charles Kelly. Salt Lake City: University of Utah Press, 1984.

———. *Writings of John D. Lee.* Edited by Samuel Nyall Henrie. Tucson, Ariz.: Hats Off Books, 2001.

Michener, James A. *Centennial.* New York: Fawcett Crest, 1974.

Moorman, John R. H. *A History of the Church in England.* 3rd ed. Harrisburg, Penn.: Morehouse Publishing, 1980.

Morgan, Kenneth O., ed. *The Oxford History of Britain.* Updated ed. Oxford: Oxford University Press, 1999.

Moynihan, Ruth B., Susan Armitage, and Christiane Fischer Dichamp, eds. 2nd ed. *So Much to Be Done: Women Settlers on the Mining and Ranching Frontier.* Lincoln: University of Nebraska Press, 1998.

Mulder, William. *Homeward to Zion: The Mormon Migration from Scandinavia.* Minneapolis: University of Minnesota Press, 1957.

Myres, Sandra L. *Westering Women and the Frontier Experience, 1800–1915.* Albuquerque: University of New Mexico Press, 1982.

Peterson, John Alton. *Utah's Black Hawk War.* Salt Lake City: University of Utah Press, 1998.

Phillips, Kevin. *The Cousins' Wars: Religion, Politics and the Triumph of Anglo-America.* New York: Basic Books, 1999.

Piercy, Frederick Hawkins. *Route from Liverpool to Great Salt Lake Valley.* Edited by Fawn M. Brodie. Cambridge, Mass.: Belknap Press / Harvard University Press, 1962.

Quiett, Glenn Chesney. *They Built the West: An Epic of Rails and Cities.* New York: D. Appleton-Century, 1934.

Reisner, Marc. *Cadillac Desert: The American West and Its Disappearing Water.* New York: Viking, 1986.

———. *Building and Breaking Families in the American West.* Albuquerque: University of New Mexico Press, 1996.

Riley, Glenda. *Women and Indians on the Frontier, 1825–1915.* Albuquerque: University of New Mexico Press, 1984.

Schlissel, Lillian, Byrd Gibbens, and Elizabeth Hampsten, eds. *Far from Home: Families of the Westward Journey.* Lincoln: University of Nebraska Press, 1989.

Schlissel, Lillian, Vicki L. Ruiz, and Janice Monk, eds. *Western Women: Their Land, Their Lives.* Albuquerque: University of New Mexico Press, 1988.

Seagraves, Anne. *High-Spirited Women of the West.* Lakeport, Calif.: Wesanne Publications, 1992.

Snow, Eliza R. *The Personal Writings of Eliza Roxcy Snow.* Edited by Maureen Ursenbach. Salt Lake City: University of Utah Press, 1995.

———. *Saints on the Seas: A Maritime History of Mormon Migration, 1830–1890.* Salt Lake City: University of Utah Press, 1983.

Sonne, Conway B. *Ships, Saints, and Mariners: A Maritime Encyclo-*

pedia of Mormon Migration, 1830–1890. Salt Lake City: University of Utah Press, 1987.

Stenhouse, Fanny (Mrs. T.B.H). *Tell It All: The Story of a Life's Experience in Mormonism; An Autobiography*. Hartford, Conn.: A. D. Worthington, 1874.

Stenhouse, T.B.H. *The Rocky Mountain Saints: A Full and Complete History of the Mormons, From the First Vision of Joseph Smith to the Last Courtship of Brigham Young*. London: Ward, Lock & Tyler, 1871.

Stratton, Joanna L. *Pioneer Women: Voices from the Kansas Frontier*. New York: Simon & Schuster / Touchstone Books, 1982.

Sykes, Stephen, John Booty, and Jonathan Knight, eds. rev. ed. *The Study of Anglicanism*. London: SPCK; Philadelphia, Fortress Press, 1998.

Taylor, Samuel W. *The Last Pioneer: John Taylor, a Mormon Prophet*. Salt Lake City: Signature Books, 1976.

Twain, Mark. *Roughing It*. 1872. New York: Viking Penguin, 1987.

Udall, Stewart L. *The Forgotten Founders: Rethinking the History of the Old West*. Washington, D.C.: Island Press, 2002.

Vidler, Alec R. *Witness to the Light: F. D. Maurice's Message for Today*. New York: Charles Scribner's Sons, 1948.

Walker, Ronald W., and Doris R. Dant, eds. *Nearly Everything Imaginable: The Everyday Life of Utah's Mormon Pioneers*. Provo, Utah: Brigham Young University Press, 1999.

Ward, Maria. *The Mormon Wife: A Life Story of the Sacrifices, Sorrows, and Sufferings of Woman; A Narrative of Many Years' Personal Experience, by the Wife of a Mormon Elder, Recently from Utah*. Hartford, Conn.: Hartford Publishing, 1873.

Weiner, Margery. *The French Exiles, 1789–1815*. London: John Murray, 1960.

Wise, William. *Massacre at Mountain Meadows: An American Legend and a Monumental Crime*. 1976. Lincoln, Nebraska: iUniverse.com, Inc., 2000.

Woodham Smith, Cecil. *The Great Hunger: Ireland 1845–1849.* London: Penguin Books, 1991.

Wright, Louis B., and H. T. Swedenberg, Jr. *The American Tradition.* New York: F. S. Crofts and Company, 1944.

SELECTED PERIODICAL AND NEWSPAPER ACCOUNTS

Aird, Polly. "Escape from Zion: The United States Army Escort of Mormon Apostates, 1859." *Nevada Historical Society Quarterly* (fall 2001).

Dickens, Charles. "The Uncommercial Traveller." *All the Year Round* (July 4, 1863).

"Portrait of a Danish Family." *Daughters of the Utah Pioneers* (March and April 1981).

MANUSCRIPTS

Edwards, Marianne. Letters, 1855–1866. Manuscript Resources on Baton Rouge History, Special Collections, Louisiana State University Libraries.

ACKNOWLEDGMENTS

I have been gathering information on Jean Rio for decades—beginning years before I had any idea how I might put the information to use. I am deeply grateful for the assistance I received from librarians and archivists in England, France, Denmark, Scotland, California, and Utah. From the tiny Antioch Historical Society to the imposing British Museum, from the volunteer-based Daughters of the Utah Pioneers to the esoteric maritime division of the Library of Congress, my inquiries met with the most professional and courteous response.

I communicated with dozens of Jean Rio's descendants, but I want especially to thank my very "distant" cousins: Jeffrey Johnson, Kenvin Lyman, Barbara Baker, Robert Gill, David Seegmiller, and David Neighbor.

I am deeply indebted to my agent, Gloria Loomis, a dear friend and my most staunch supporter. Jonathan Segal at Knopf has worked his magic with Jean Rio as he has for me so many times before.

Once again, I have Roger Morris to thank for his generosity in taking time from his own overwhelming writing schedule to serve as my first reader.

Finally, my family is the light that shows me the way. My parents, Ralph and Sara Denton, are my solid and enthusiastic backers, always there to make my life easier as rolling deadlines loom. My beautiful sons—Ralph, Grant, and Carson—are a daily reminder of what is important and why history matters.

INDEX

A NOTE ABOUT THE AUTHOR

Sally Denton is the author of *American Massacre: The Tragedy at Mountain Meadows, September 1857; The Bluegrass Conspiracy: An Inside Story of Power, Greed, Drugs, and Murder,* and, with Roger Morris, *The Money and the Power: The Making of Las Vegas and Its Hold on America, 1947–2000.* She is an award-winning investigative reporter; her journalism has appeared in *American Heritage, The New York Times, The Washington Post,* and *Salon.* She received the Western Heritage Award in 2002 and 2004, and a Lannan Literary grant in 2000. She lives in the Southwest with her three sons.

A NOTE ON THE TYPE

This book was set in Minion, a typeface produced by the Adobe Corporation specifically for the Macintosh personal computer, and released in 1990. Designed by Robert Slimbach, Minion combines the classic characteristics of old style faces with the full compliment of weights required for modern typesetting.

COMPOSED BY NORTH MARKET STREET GRAPHICS,

LANCASTER, PENNSYLVANIA

PRINTED AND BOUND BY R. R. DONNELLY & SONS,

HARRISONBURG, VIRGINIA

DESIGNED BY ROBERT C. OLSSON

MAP BY DAVID LINDROTH, INC.